Indians on the Game

Indians on the Game

Wayne Stewart

GRAY & COMPANY, PUBLISHERS
CLEVELAND

*To my mother-in-law, Pearl Panich, to her daughter Nancy
(my wife), and to her two grandsons, Sean and Scott (my sons,
and two fine baseball players themselves).*

Gray & Company, Publishers
1588 E. 40th Street
Cleveland, Ohio 44103
www.grayco.com

Special permission was given by Baseball Digest and Beckett
Publications to reprint some material used in this book. Used
with permission of Sterling Publishing Co., Inc., NY, NY from
Baseball Oddities: Bizarre Plays & Other Funny Stuff by
Wayne Stewart, © 1998 by Wayne Stewart. Used with permission of Sterling Publishing Co., Inc., NY, NY from Baseball bafflers by Wayne Stewart, © 1999 by Wayne Stewart. Used with
permission of Sterling Publishing Co., Inc., NY, NY from
Baseball Puzzlers: You Make the Call by Wayne Stewart, ©
2000 by Wayne Stewart.

Library of Congress Cataloging-in-Publication Data
Stewart, Wayne
 Indians on the Game / Wayne Stewart.
p. cm.
ISBN 1-886228-44-2
1. Baseball—Miscellanea. 2. Cleveland Indians (Baseball
team)—Interviews. I. Title.
GV873 .S86 2001
796.357'64'0977132--dc21
2001000343

ISBN 1-886228-44-2

Printed in the United States of America
First Printing

CONTENTS

INTRODUCTION

This book gives an insider's view of the game of baseball. Actually, many insiders' views, because even veteran ballplayers who've been teammates for years have different opinions about how the game should be played. That's part of what makes baseball so much fun to discuss—there's plenty to disagree on.

A lot goes on in major league baseball that fans never get to see firsthand—during game preparation, in the dugout and the clubhouse, on the road, and at home after the game.

Luckily, most ballplayers love to talk about baseball and are willing to go on the record and share their experience with the rest of us.

There are already lots of books about baseball, of course, including several collections of quotations by players. But one thing you'll notice when flipping through them: they include relatively few quotes by Cleveland Indians players.

I happen to think it's a lot of fun—and often more enlightening—to hear the opinions of players I'm most familiar with. Players I've watched over the years, read about in the paper, heard stories about. That's why this book collects quotations about baseball by Cleveland Indians players past and present.

Many of these quotations I culled from back issues of local papers and baseball publications and from several excellent books written about the Indians over the years. Many more quotes I got during my own firsthand interviews.

The questions don't cover every aspect of the game of baseball. But they cover a lot of the topics that I know baseball fans are curious about.

The answers aren't necessarily the only answers or the "right" ones. But they are representative of what many other players think and feel. Obviously no one player can speak for all of baseball, but these candid comments are packed full of honesty, insights, and even wisdom at times.

The players quoted include journeymen as well as stars.

I chose the men and women quoted here for a variety of reasons. In some cases, because they represent a certain aspect of baseball. Bill Selby, for instance, is a perfect spokesperson to illustrate what life is like for a young player who's not yet established himself in the big leagues. Sure, he's no longer an Indian, but that's part of the game, too. Andrea Pacione Thome could reveal what it's like to be married to a star player. Many were chosen because they are particularly articulate, insightful, or accessible. Some are quoted frequently because they've gone out of their way to make their opinions known as a matter of record—Bob Feller is a prime example.

I hope their words will help fans to better understand how players think about their game, to see what it's like in the Cleveland clubhouse, hear what it's like to be married to a ballplayer, find out more about the game-day routine of a vendor or groundskeeper, or peek at the life of baseball announcers. And, I hope they'll simply be fun to read.

So, here now are the words, wit, and wisdom of many Indians on the game. Enjoy!

Indians on the Game

On the Field

HITTING

What kind of hitters cause the most problems for pitchers?

According to Bob Feller, **"The hitters who don't swing hard are the toughest to get out**. . . . The most dangerous are those who just meet the ball. They can turn a pitcher's win into a loss at light speed."** [*Bob Feller's Little Black Book*]

What must a hitter do to be successful in the long run?

Mike Hargrove said that the two keys to becoming a big league success are intelligence and a willingness to adjust. He said, **"This game is built on adjustment—constant adjustment. Talent will take you so far**. That's why you see guys do well for a couple of years, and then drop out of sight. You have to be willing to adjust." [*Baseball Digest*, 7/94]

How long does it take young hitters to adapt to the ways pitchers try to work them?

Former Indians manager Doc Edwards said, "There was

an accepted theory that a player needed 1,500 to 1,600 at bats in the minors before he'd be ready to handle the adjustments he'd have to make to hit major league pitching."
[*Baseball Digest*, 7/94]

"What takes time is to learn how to have that constant approach," said Travis Fryman. "How to put the ups and downs behind you, and not ride your emotions so much as a young player or any young person does. They're very controlled by their emotions. As an old player you learn how to even those things out a little bit."

What wears a hitter out more, the physical or mental aspects of the game?

Fryman said it is very difficult to give 100 percent mentally: "That's the challenge of baseball—the day-in, day-out ability to mentally prepare yourself to play. It's the hardest skill to learn in Major League Baseball. That's why it takes young players several years before they become consistent players. . . . It's a learning process; it takes time and patience on the part of an organization, the individual, and fans as well."

How do hitters use videotapes to improve their performance?

On video, "You see how you're hitting when you're going good or going bad, and you can make corrections," said Albert Belle. And, he added, "The more you see a pitcher, the more confident you are." Before one game against Seattle, he gave an example. "Today we're facing Brian

Fisher, so we have a tape of his last outing against us. You get a picture of how he'll face us today."

When a player steps out of the batter's box, is he actually thinking about the at bat or is he simply stalling for time?

"Most of the time," said Travis Fryman, "you're thinking or calming yourself down a little bit, trying to back off a little, or just trying to relax a little in that situation. You might feel tense up there, or maybe you think a guy's going to throw a pitch here so you're hashing over some things. But **very few guys are just stalling; there's a thought process behind it**."

How does patience—taking more pitches—help not only a batter but also the rest of the team?

In 1999 Roberto Alomar saw more pitches than any other Indian (2,946 in all). He said, "I've always been a patient hitter. I like to make the pitchers work. I don't like to give him any easy outs. **If I can make him throw me four, five, or six pitches and the other guys can do the same, that pitcher is going to be tired by the sixth or seventh inning**."

He added, "Now, if a pitcher is throwing strikes, it's a different story." During the 1999 season, he thought pitchers were throwing more first-pitch strikes to him. For at bats where Alomar made contact with the first pitch, his average was a lusty .583 (on 21 for 36). [*Plain Dealer*, 2/26/00]

How do hitters decide whether or not to take a pitch or two before swinging?

Infield and first base coach Brian Graham said, "The game situation dictates your approach offensively. With some pitchers, even if Pedro Martinez is late into a game, you want to get a pitch you can hit. Because if he gets ahead of you, he has such an array of pitches that you're in trouble. So, you better get a pitch to hit, and if it happens to be the first pitch, you better take your shot at the first pitch. He's got a lot better chance of nibbling once he gets ahead of you in that situation.

"You definitely take a strike on Jose Mesa because his out pitch is the fastball, and his get-ahead pitch is the fastball. He's got to get it over the plate, so you're still going to get a chance at the fastball later in the count.

"It depends on who the pitcher is and who's hitting behind you, too. If you're down at the end of the order and you have a guy who's not going to hit a home run, then it's a tough call."

What kind of pitch makes a hitter's eyes light up?

Chris Chambliss said he always preferred sliders, because with a faster pitch the batter "doesn't have to supply all the power" for a long shot. He said, "Batters want something fairly fast. Obviously they don't want a Nolan Ryan fastball because he throws *really* hard, but I would actually say even a change-up that's thrown high and a little too hard becomes a batting practice–type fastball. That can go the farthest, too."

Joe Carter said that contrary to what many fans think, "The hanging curveball goes farther than a [hard] fastball or a knuckleball. **Anything off speed is going to go a little bit farther than a regular fastball. A curveball especially is going to go the farthest**. Those are the ones that you hit high up in the air, and they tend to go far because the wind kind of catches them a little more."

How can a hitter beat an infield shift?

Batting coach Clarence Jones said, "**It's easy to beat the shift. All you got to do is hit it in the stands.**" [*Plain Dealer*, 4/15/00]

Have players always been easily outraged when a pitcher throws them in tight?

That's true today, but Lou Boudreau said things weren't always this way. "Today's batter gets mad at the first pitch that comes near him. He's ready to fight. When I was playing, they threw at you to see what kind of man you were."

Is it reasonable for a hitter to charge the mound after being hit by a pitch?

"Sometimes it's irrational," said Paul Shuey, "but also I know just from when I used to hit, if somebody throws at my head, what happens is you get scared. And when you get scared, you have [one of] two reactions—either you get scared and you stay scared, or you get really, really pissed. And when you get really, really pissed, watch out, man. I'm coming at you; I'm coming at anybody. I know because **I've had balls come right at my head, lost my temper, and run after my high school coach for throwing it in B.P. It's just an instinct thing**."

Can too much weight-training hurt a batter's swing?

Marty Cordova said he bulked up in 2000 when he was with the Blue Jays. "I was more muscular then, actually I was muscle-bound," he said. "Now, I have more bat speed and I can make better use of my hands. I feel skinnier and faster."

He dropped about 15 pounds before trying out with the Indians. "It's hard to get stronger without getting bigger. I did try to get stronger, and it got to the point where it was just too much." [*Elyria Chronicle Telegram*, 4/22/01]

He said he also lost weight "so the inside pitch wouldn't tie me up." [*The Lorain Morning Journal*, 4/23/01]

POWER HITTING

If a power hitter has no protection in the lineup (i.e., other power hitters batting after him), how does that change his approach to hitting?

In 1984 Andre Thornton was the only serious threat in the Indians' lineup. He said, "With a runner on base, I have to take a chance. **In those instances, I'm not thinking home run, just base hit. But they're counting on me to pick up the**

tough runs here." He risked going after some bad—but not terrible—pitches, and it worked. He swatted 33 homers to tie a career high, drove in 99 runs, and still hit nearly 20 points above his lifetime average. [*The Sporting News*, 7/23/84]

Is power hitting a feast-or-famine occupation?

Moody outfielder Albert Belle said, "When I hit home runs, they come in streaks. That's the way most power hitters are." [*Baseball Digest*, 7/94]

In general, should a batter try *to hit home runs?*

Rico Carty said he just "tried to hit the ball hard." He wanted to hit hard line drives; if they carried out of the park, great.

David Justice, felt the same way. **"I've never considered myself a home run hitter,**" he said in 1994, coming off a 40-home-run season, **"but I can't convince people of that anymore** ... I've always felt I'm a line drive hitter with the potential to hit home runs." [*Baseball Digest*, c. 3/94]

In 1994, Kenny Lofton hit 12 homers after hitting only 6 in his previous two years. He believes his home run output is what helped him make the All Star team, but, he added, "My one goal . . . was not to hit homers, but hit the ball hard enough so they couldn't play me real shallow in the outfield." [*Baseball Digest*, 4/95]

Do hitters consciously try to hit a home run sometimes anyway?

Recalling his record fourth homer in a game, Rocky Colavito said, "I came up in the ninth inning, I was the first batter. My roomie, Herb Score, called to me, 'O.K. now, don't fool around, roomie, go for number four.'

"I said, 'Are you kidding? I haven't even had four *hits* in a couple of weeks!'"

He also told Score he'd be content with a single to give him a 4-for-4 night, but Score said, "Bull. Go up and do it."

Sure enough, he did it, saying, "I hit that one the furthest of all." Up to that moment only Lou Gehrig had ever hit four consecutive homers during a nine-inning contest.

On the other hand, there's Alan Bannister. On July 14, 1983, he hit a home run in the 10th inning to win a game against the Kansas City Royals. Even though it was only his 15th career homer, reporters asked Bannister if he was "thinking home run" when he stepped up to the plate. He replied, **"Hey, if a guy's got eight years in the big leagues and less than 20 homers, thinking home run is not a very smart move."** [*The Sporting News*, 8/1/83]

What about a hitter who is "in the zone"—in the middle of a home-run streak. Should he try to hit one out?

Some do, but, Tony Horton said he learned a simple lesson, "Just try to get good wood on the ball."

On May 24, 1970, he became one of only 10 players in Cleveland history to hit three homers in a game. In his last at bat, a home run would've won the game for the Indians and tied him with Colavito and a small group of other men with four home runs in a game.

"That's what I did wrong," said Horton. **"I've told myself a thousand times, 'Don't try to hit a home run because you never do when you try**. Just try to meet the ball.'

"But, no. I'm a real blockhead. I go up there swinging from my fanny. It was the worst thing I could have done." While he said that he got a good pitch to hit from Lindy McDaniel of the Yankees on a 2–0 delivery, "It was so good it surprised me. It was right down the pipe. I really jumped at the ball," he said. He popped it up. [*The Sporting News*, 6/6/70]

CLUTCH HITTING

Why are players who can spray hits to various fields so valuable?

Onetime Cleveland manager Doc Edwards loved how players like Pat Tabler "use the whole field." Edwards said, "I'll tell you one thing: If I'm an opposing manager, I want to see Tabler at the plate only when [nothing but] a grand slam will beat me. If all it's going to take is a single, I'm probably in trouble." [*The Sporting News*, 3/21/88]

BUNTING

Why is the sacrifice bunt so important?

David Segui said, "You see Robbie Alomar bunt with no

one giving him a sign, to put the guy behind him in a better situation. When one guy does that, it goes right down the lineup. When a team doesn't do that, a certain selfishness sets in.

"If there's a guy on second base, everyone can't go up there saying, 'I've got to drive that guy in.' If one guy doesn't try to move the runner over, the guy behind him is going to say, 'If you're not going to move him over for me, I'm not going to do it for you.'"** [*Plain Dealer*, 9/16/00]

SLUMPS

Do players have special ways of breaking out of slumps?

According to Minnie Minoso's onetime roommate Vic Power, Minoso believed in voodoo. Power was quoted as saying, "When he went 0 for 4 he'd wear his uniform in the shower so he could drown the spirits." [*This Side of Cooperstown*]

Can a player break out of a slump by simply trying harder?

"Matt Williams said something that I thought was very profound in a Yogi Berra–like way," recalled radio announcer Matt Underwood. "He said, **When I'm really struggling, I have to try easier**. Everybody always says you have to try harder. In baseball, if you try harder, you tense up, you put too much pressure on yourself. The key is to just back off, take a deep breath, and try easier.'"

DESIGNATED HITTER

Isn't it easier to be the designated hitter, because you don't have to play the field?

Jim Thome doesn't think so. "DHing itself is not the thing that bothers me, it's the length of time between at bats. It makes me respect bench players. You get an at bat and might not get another chance to hit for 40 minutes. You've got to keep loose because you're not in the game."

[*Plain Dealer*, 9/15/00]

Do pitchers like not having to bat because of the American League designated hitter rule?

Steve Karsay said he prefers the National League approach, where "the pitcher gets up there and stays in the game and hits. Sometimes he depends on himself to get a bunt down to keep himself in the game. **I think it's just the fundamentals of baseball that if you can have the pitchers do the things the other guys are doing, be an all-around player, it makes you a better athlete**."

Dwight Gooden, former National League Rookie of the Year and Cy Young Award winner before playing for the Indians, said about the designated hitter rule, "I'd get rid of it, that's the one thing about the game I'd change."

BASE RUNNING

When beating out an infield hit, is it faster to run through the bag at first or slide head first?

Most experts tell you never to slide. Omar Vizquel said, "I believe it's faster running through the bag, but Robbie [Alomar] doesn't think so. He's been using that [head first slide] play since he came into the big leagues."

Alomar said, "A lot of people have told me I shouldn't do it, but it's the way I play the game." [*Plain Dealer*, 6/6/99]

Are players fairly criticized for not running hard on an easy out?

"I guess when you have speed, they expect you to run all the time," said speedy outfielder Rick Manning. "I never made excuses. I know when I didn't run something out. But **some of these home run hitters, they would pop up and they wouldn't even drag their fat asses halfway to first base and nothing was ever said about them.**" [*The Curse of Rocky Colavito*]

Does a player investigate the ballpark to learn information that might help him when he's on the base paths?

Many players, especially when they are new to the league, or when they first visit a new park, will try to learn as much as they can. Russell Branyan said he'd even check out the makeup of the backstop to see if the ball will bounce off that area and ricochet back to the catcher, or if it will die. "Oh, definitely," he said, "because one run means a lot in games. Kenny Lofton scored on a wild pitch that put us ahead [in one game]—one run can mean a ball game."

And, he said, "Each ball park has its own rules—if you can go down into a dugout and catch a ball or if you have to stand on the top, if you can go into it and then come out and throw the ball."

What's the hardest thing to learn about the running game?
"You can't teach speed—either you have it or you don't," said Kenny Lofton.

What talent makes one speedy athlete a better baserunner than others?
"Great first-step acceleration," said coach Dave Nelson.

What factors does a third-base coach consider before deciding whether to send a runner home or stop him?
"Late in the game, for instance, you might be more aggressive," said Joel Skinner. "You're facing a tough pitcher, they're in the back of their bullpen and matching up. You can't be sure if another opportunity will arise, so you have to maximize it."

Weather matters, too. "Damp or wet conditions lead to wet grass, which could slow down the outfielder and hamper the grip on the ball. At the same time, a line drive into wet grass could skid, reaching the outfielder quicker."

And where the Indians are in their batting order can be

crucial. "If we've got Omar Vizquel on second," he said, "with less than two outs and Robbie Alomar hits a ball sharply to left, I'm going to be careful because we've got Juan Gonzalez coming up, and Ellis Burks and Jim Thome after that. You always need to look at least one batter ahead." [*Plain Dealer*, 4/14/01]

What does a player think about when considering stretching a single into a double?

"First," said Kenny Lofton, "I think about where I hit the ball and is it still rolling when I hit first base. Then a lot of my decision to try for second base depends on how I feel running that day. If I'm sore, I might not do it."

BASE STEALING

Does his position in the batting order affect how often a player steals?

Robbie Alomar said, "Hitting third I pick my spot to steal bases." He said he is more selective when he has sluggers like Manny Ramirez, David Justice, and Jim Thome batting after him. "You have to give them a chance, especially in a close game, to hit a home run."

How does a coach help a runner improve his base-stealing technique?

Dave Nelson kept statistics on all American League pitchers. "[We] go over pitchers' tendencies—go over my reports on their moves and 'times' to the plate," he said, referring to the amount of time it takes a pitcher to deliver the ball to the plate. The slower the time, the better the chance to steal a base, not on the catcher, but on a lethargic pitcher.

Nelson said that in the case of a speedster like Kenny Lofton, "I try to show him what to look for so he can know when the pitcher is going home and know his setup. **Anyone can key on, say, a pitcher's shoulders. I want Kenny to know from just the pitcher's set**. You can read his habits. There are ways he'll set up when he's going home, and when he's throwing over."

Can base-stealers go through a slump?

Sure. Manager Mike Hargrove said Kenny Lofton once was "in a base-running slump [partly because] he's been guessing a lot lately, and he's been guessing wrong."

CATCHER

What do catchers learn about catching from their pitchers?

"I think I learned the most . . . from the veteran pitchers," said Al Lopez. "**You have to learn to think like a pitcher, how to set the batters up, and keep them off balance**." Lopez said Dolf Luque was the smartest pitcher he ever caught. "He'd shake me off until I knew exactly what to signal for. After a while I was thinking just like he was. Sometimes I'd have to signal him to pretend to shake me off, just to keep them guessing. We'd also sit together on the bench when our team was batting. So we had a perfect understanding. I learned that that was a big part of catching—getting the pitchers' confidence. If you have that confidence, and, of course, if you can call a good game—you need that to maintain confidence—you're a great asset to the pitcher. He doesn't have to worry about thinking then. . . . He can concentrate on putting the ball in the mitt. [*Baseball for the Love of It*]

Does a catcher delight in working a no-hitter as much as the pitcher who is responsible for the gem?

Gary Alexander, who caught John Montefusco's no-hitter, said it was his greatest big league thrill. "I even felt like I threw it.

"I mentioned to each hitter when they came up to the plate [in the final inning]: 'Don't be a bad sport and try to bunt, swing away.' The last hitter was Jerry Royster and I said to him, 'Please don't bunt. Earn the hit, but don't bunt on us.'" [*Baseball Digest*, 11/79]

Do catchers have the attitude that they play an elite position?

Duke Sims, who caught for the Indians from 1964 to 1970, joked about his position, "I didn't start catching until I was a senior in high school. . . I was the only guy dumb enough to go behind the plate." Yet he took pride in his position. Sims also teased that **"the catcher and the pitcher are the only guys who earn their pay. Hell, anybody who plays first**

base is stealing money. If you take enough ground balls, you've got to get to the point where you can be a pretty good infielder, and the same thing goes for an outfielder, if he takes enough fly balls." [*The Sporting News*, 8/22/70]

Who makes the decision when pitcher and catcher disagree about what pitch to throw?

   "**It's really the pitcher's game**," said catcher Jim Hegan. "If he doesn't feel good about a pitch you call, chances are he won't throw it well." [*Tribe Memories*]

How heavily do pitchers rely on their catchers?

   If he's a good catcher, the answer is "a lot." Scott Scudder was elated when he came to Cleveland from Cincinnati, saying it was great working with Sandy Alomar and Joel Skinner. "They're big targets and they know the game well. It's good to have leadership behind the plate."

INFIELD

Is it difficult for an infielder to switch to a new position? Shouldn't a third baseman be able to play first base—the position that's the mirror image of third—with ease?

   Third baseman Travis Fryman had to play first base in an interleague game against the Cincinnati Reds during the 2000 season because manager Charlie Manuel made so many pitching changes.

   "It was a good idea for a little while," said Manuel, "but

I'd just as soon see him play third base." Meanwhile, others weren't so kind. Fryman said, "Thome said I looked pretty good and Richie [Sexson] said I looked like crap. Richie's a little more blunt." [*Elyria Chronicle Telegram*, June 12, 2000]

Mark Lewis, who has played both sides on the infield, said, "It is different, especially at the big league level. You get different angles of the ball" coming off the bat when playing the two sides.

Do players resent another man who took their job, forcing them to move to either a different defensive position or to the bench?

In 1970, Eddie Leon, then 24 years old, lost his starting shortstop job to Jack Heidemann, 21. Heidemann said during an interview in May of 1970, "They moved Eddie to second base at Portland last year, but he still had hopes of playing shortstop up here [with the Indians]. I know Eddie didn't like being moved, and I don't blame him. I would have felt the same way. I'm jealous of anyone playing my position, too."

Leon said, "I never had any hard feelings toward him, but I did resent being shifted to second base because of him." [*The Sporting News*, 8/29/70]

What physical traits are required of a good infielder?

"If you're going to play the infield, you need to have good footwork," said Omar Vizquel. **"Your feet and legs are the start of good defense."** [*Omar Vizquel, the Man with the Golden Glove*]

How do infielders use "decoy" moves to trick baserunners?

Roberto Alomar said, "We try to do it when a guy's running and somebody hits a fly ball. If the runner doesn't see it, we try to deke him, acting like we're going to make a double play. Then the outfielder can throw him out at first base."

Or, said Alomar, "If the guy's running and the batter hits the ball behind the runner, I can try to deke him that I caught the ball and I'm going to throw it to the shortstop." He pantomimed a phantom catch and throw. "The shortstop makes it look like he's going to make a double play, so the guy thinks I caught it and he's going to slide. So now he's not going to make it to third base on the ball [a clean hit] to right field.

"Now, if it's a fly ball to right field, and he doesn't know where the ball is, we're going to try to deke him, see if we can make him look for the ball. If he doesn't know where the ball really is many times the right fielder has already caught the ball, and he can throw him out at first base."

Alomar said the runner must "peek to home plate. If he doesn't do this, and you can see that as an infielder, you know the runner doesn't know where the ball is—he has no clue. Now he's got to look at the coaches, but some of the guys can't hear them—it's not easy out there, it's so loud. If he doesn't look at the coaches and doesn't see what's going on, you try to decoy him and we can get a double play. Maybe it's going to work 5 percent of the time, maybe 2 percent, but it could be good."

Do fielders ever pull the old hidden ball trick anymore?

Matt Williams, Gold Glove third baseman, was quite skilled at that particular trick. In 1997 he was playing third base when he got the idea of trying the hidden ball trick during a game against the Kansas City Royals. Sandy Alomar said, "He told the guy [base runner Jed Hansen] to get off the base so he could clean it. He was a rookie. Williams tagged the guy and he was out; they were pretty upset about that."

OUTFIELD

What makes a good center fielder?

Kenny Lofton said speed allows him to simplify his approach to defense: "That's what I do most comfortably, flat out go get the ball."

He said his defense was "a combination of my jump on the ball and my speed. My arm's good enough. I just try to be consistent with my throwing. If I can get a jump on the ball and get my body angled in the right direction, my arm's right there." [Associated Press, 3/8/92]

Is there a big difference between playing left and right fields, or should a professional be able to play both sides?

In March of 2000, David Justice had just switched sides. "I am still learning how to play left field. I am still learning the ins and outs of left field. **The difference in playing in left and right field is huge**. The ball comes off the bat differently. I never even stood in left field all the years I played for the Braves. I will be the first to admit I am not an accomplished left fielder yet." [*Plain Dealer*, 3/23/00]

Later in the season when right-fielder Manny Ramirez was out with a strained hamstring, Justice returned to his natural position. He said, "It's like if you go to another country and they drive on the left side of the road. I can do it, but I might make a couple of mistakes." [*Elyria Chronicle Telegram*, 6/11/00]

Russell Branyan had the added difficulty of switching from third base to right field in the 2000 season. "They say left field is tougher than right," he said, "but I like left field a little bit better than right because that's my side of the diamond. They say you have more right-handed hitters who hit the ball hard; left-handers are slicing the ball. So, you're going to see more balls pulled at you with top spin than you would in right field simply because there are more right-handed hitters in the game.

"Right-handed power hitters hit the ball hard with top spin, hard with back spin—it depends on how they catch it. You gotta be able to read the ball. You have some shorter throws in left field, but you still gotta make better reads, so I could see left field being the tougher position," he concluded. [*Plain Dealer*, 7/17/00]

How does an outfielder decide where to position himself against various hitters?

Mainly from scouting reports and advice from experienced players. Brett Butler once came across a scouting report saying he had trouble going back on fly balls. Instead of getting angry about the report, he changed his technique. "Hey," he said, "**some of those scouts know what they're talking about**. So, I moved back 10 feet. I'd rather give up an occasional single that falls in front of me than a double or triple over my head." [*The Sporting News*, 7/8/85]

At a new ballpark, will a player check out the outfield and the walls to see how he will play balls hit to him?

If he's smart, he will. Russell Branyan said, "You got so many new ballparks built now, and the ballparks are built differently now—they have different shapes and configurations of the outfield wall. You've got different areas to work with in foul grounds."

Branyan said the Indians will take a ball to the outfield and throw it off the wall to see how a baseball will play off various surfaces—especially in all the new parks being erected of late. He said he does this "just to see what kind of bounce you get."

"That ballpark in Texas, right field's kinda got some different angles, and the fence isn't true all the way around. Over in Houston they've got a flagpole in center field, so you gotta watch out."

PITCHING

How important is mental preparation for a pitcher?

Cameron Cairncross said, "It's pretty big at this level. It goes a long way. You really got to sit down and think because there are so many guys competing for your job, so you've got to give yourself every chance when you go out there." Cairncross feels one of the best ways is to be mentally tough.

Do pitchers watch their previous performance for ways to improve next time?

Cairncross said it helps to study charts and videotapes. "I like to see where my pitches were—if I thought they were close. I want to see [what] the action is on the ball. Yeah, video's a big thing nowadays. You can pick up a little flaw in your mechanics."

What separates an average major league pitcher from a star?

"In the majors, the physical part of the game is over—it becomes mental," said Rick Sutcliffe, a onetime Cy Young Award winner. "Baseball is a game of adjustments. Those who make adjustments are a success." He added that in order to make changes from, for example, one at bat to another, or even from one trip into a city to the next to face a given pitcher, "You have to have a good memory."

What do pitchers learn by "charting" the pitches of another pitcher from the bench?

"I think it's really so you're watching the game, so you're not just sitting there BS-ing on the bench," said Cameron Cairncross. But, he said, if a pitcher is working the next game, he should be especially attentive the day before.

"Every pitcher is different . . . but you can watch the way he sets up to get to his pitch, you watch how he works the hitter. That gives you an opportunity to see if the guy's going to lunge out and try to pull that pitch or is he standing up straight. Should I knock him off the plate? It gives you a bit of an idea [how to pitch them]."

Can the Little League–type advice of "just throw the ball over the plate, let them hit it, and allow your defense to do the job" work on a major league level?

Dave Burba tried it in one game against Seattle during the 2000 season. "After I got that 9–0 lead, I threw batting practice. I didn't throw many splits. I didn't throw many curveballs. I threw batting practice."

He admitted he was a bit surprised by his success, saying, "I'm sitting on the bench after I struck out Rickey Henderson on a batting-practice fastball, and I wondered, **'Why can't it be like this all the time?' You spend all this time in between starts working on mechanics and your breaking ball, and then you win a game by basically throwing batting practice.**"

[*Plain Dealer*, 8/21/00]

Shortly after Burba's outing, Finley turned in a similar performance. This time Charlie Manuel observed, "Chuck Finley did a good job. He threw the ball over the plate and let them hit it. He was not trying for strikeouts. He was letting the fielders do their job."

Commenting on that September 1, 2000, showing,

Finley said, "I tend to go out and try to work corners, but tonight I wanted to take a little more of the plate and keep the ball down." He threw to the middle of the plate instead of trying to be too cute with his location, and it worked.

[*Plain Dealer*, 9/2/00]

Dave Otto said he used to let his defense make plays behind him because he wasn't, by and large, a flame thrower. "Sometimes," he said, "I can throw pretty hard, but overall **I just let them put the ball in play and try to get the grounder**."

Do pitchers ever feel like every pitch they throw is going to be a strike, that they're just locked in on their target?

Justin Speier said, "When a pitcher's in a groove, or in the zone, every pitch you throw, you know where it's going—you know what location it's going to. It seems like it's automatic, the ball's going to go there, but that only happens once in awhile."

Which are the best "hitters' counts" and "pitchers' counts"?

Speier said, "The best hitters' counts are 2–0, 3–0, 3–1, and 2–1, and the best pitchers' counts are 0–2, 1–2. When the hitters are ahead in the count they can look for one specific area and zone in on it, looking for the ball there. Now, when the hitter is 0–2 or 1–2, then he's going to be more defensive and have to expand his zone a little bit more." Expanding that zone means possibly chasing after a bad pitch for a strikeout.

What about when the pitcher is struggling and can't seem to find the plate—what does that feel like?

"You feel like you don't have command of your pitches," Speier said. "You might have great stuff that day, but you just don't have command of where it's going to go. You get behind in the count. You feel out of sync, you feel like everything's not working together."

What should a pitcher do to hold a runner on first base?

"Holding men on base is vital to a pitcher's success in the major leagues," said Bob Feller. "**Most pitchers feel that they have to physically throw over to first base each time they want to hold a man there. This is not true**. A pitcher should look runners back to the bag, taking his foot off the pitching rubber, and not throw until the runner is motionless or moving back toward first base." [*Bob Feller's Little Black Book*]

With so many new parks having such good hitting backdrops for batters, what advantage is left for the pitcher?

Paul Shuey said, "The only possible edge we [pitchers] might have once in awhile is when you have a five o'clock game. You get shadows coming across the field and that can be hard for a player to see." Overall, he feels, when it comes to visibility, hitters have it pretty good.

What rule change would reduce the advantage hitters have over pitchers?

Onetime Indians coach Joe Nossek said, "I'd give the pitchers a little bit of an edge by raising the mounds now. The hitters are getting so big and strong, the pitchers are falling behind a little." He thinks going back to 15-inch mounds is too drastic. First of all, he concedes, "I kinda think there might be a few mounds around a little higher than 10 inches right now." Still, he would allow all the ball-parks to nudge the mound up a bit.

Have position players ever pitched in a game?

Sure, most teams have done this on occasion over the years; after all, why waste a good bull-pen arm in a blowout? The Indians once had one of the game's most famous and prodigious home run hitters mop up.

Rocky Colavito said he got a kick out of his two pitching stints, both against the Detroit Tigers. His 1958 appearance on the mound was the only time he threw as an Indians "pitcher." His other outing came in 1968 as he wound down his career with the New York Yankees. He joked, "I pitched every 10 years."

He actually did well, with these lifetime stats: 0.00 E.R.A.; 5 ⅔ innings pitched; one hit surrendered; and two strikeouts. He was wild, though, giving up five walks. Still, he even managed to earn a victory for his 1968 perform-ance. "The win was a big thrill. I got more publicity then, than when I hit the four home runs [in a game]."

Why are fewer complete games pitched nowadays?

Complete games today are about as scarce as unicorns. Bob Feller said, "It used to be expected that a starting pitcher would pace himself and make it through the complete game if he possibly could. Nowadays the manager tells him, 'Go out and give it everything on every pitch! That's why we have a bullpen.' So after, say, six innings, the pitcher's looking over his shoulder for some relief, whether he needs it or not. In addition, my personal view is that the pitchers don't have as much stamina as they used to have."
[*Baseball for the Love of It*]

Gaylord Perry didn't want to place his fate in another pitcher's hands. In 1972, he had 40 decisions in 40 starts, going 24–16 with a league-leading 29 complete games, a total now unheard of. "We didn't have many relief pitchers in Cleveland," he said. "You just had to go out there, and if it took ten innings to do it, I took it." [*Baseball Digest*, 5/90]

How does pitching inside to hitters help the pitcher?

Bob Feller said, "The first strikeout I ever got was in July of 1936. . . . I had thrown too close to the first man I faced, and then came [Buddy] Lewis, and he was nowhere *near* the plate. He *couldn't* have hit the ball; he struck out." [*This Side of Cooperstown*]

What do pitchers think when they have a poor defense playing behind them?

David Segui said he played on teams with a weak defense, and that it affects the pitchers in a highly negative

way. **"You can see it in their eyes . . . They think they have to strike out everyone."**
[*Elyria Chronicle Telegram*, 9/17/00]

According to broadcaster Joe Tait, infielder Jack Brohamer once said, "When you made an error behind Gaylord [Perry], he would just stand on the mound and stare at you. I mean, you just wanted to shrivel up right on the spot." [*The Curse of Rocky Colavito*]

When does a pitcher come into his prime?
"A lot of guys don't learn how to pitch until they're 30, 31 years old," said Dennis Cook. "I'm learning something every day."

Bob Feller said, "In my early years I never learned to 'pitch,' because I didn't think I had to. I figured that even if I walked a few batters, I could power pitch my way out of a jam. By the late forties things were different. I'd lost a lot of my steam, and I realized I had to be a 'pitcher' out there, not just a thrower. I learned." [*Baseball for the Love of It*]

What goals do pitchers set for themselves?
"The first thing people want to hear as goals are numbers," said Scott Scudder. "But there are a lot of other factors that go along with winning and losing. **Whether I get the win or not is up to other people."** He said he just wanted to go as many innings as he could as a starter and hope the team could rally behind him and get the win for the Indians.

"I think it's important just to get the hitter out, so you

take it one pitch at a time," said a more pragmatic Dave Otto. "That relieves some of the pressure. You put other things out of your mind and concentrate on the pitch."

Jack Armstrong said, "I'm proud of just giving everything I've got every day, of my persistence, and attention to dedication day in and day out. I just want to get in the 35 or so starts they give me and give them quality starts, to try to keep the team in the game. No quitting."

Do pitchers change how they pitch to players from one at bat to the next?

"Pitching is pitching," said Scott Kamieniecki. "I have yet to hear a pitcher say he throws differently to hitters in the second or third from the way he throws to them in the seventh or eighth." [*Elyria Chronicle Telegram*, 3/25/00]

Pitching coach Dick Pole disagreed. "I would think you have to change something the second time through the lineup."

Should a pitcher change his approach when his team has a big lead?

Bob Feller said, "I'd pace myself. If I had a lead, I'd ease up. Then you can bear down on tough guys or save yourself for the next game. I didn't care about E.R.A., but it takes time to learn this. . . . The bottom line is did you win or lose. **What's more important, having a low E.R.A. or having a high one and winning**?"

Why do some pitchers tend to give up a lot of home runs?

Contrary to what some fans think, giving up homers doesn't necessarily mean the pitcher is a stiff. The man who gave up the most career homers was a huge star, Robin Roberts. The pitcher who dished up the most for a single season was ex-Indian Bert Blyleven, another legitimate star.

Dennis Cook said, "I don't like to give in to the batter, that's just my personality. I challenge them. **If they hit it, make it be a solo shot**. I can't let it bother me."

How does a young pitcher change with experience?

"You learn with experience how to take control of a game," said Charles Nagy. He said that in his first year or so, he put total faith in his catchers. "Whatever they put down, I threw, but you learn to trust yourself and your ability. You have to pitch the way you did in the minors, the way that got you here. It comes with confidence; you'll shake the catcher off. You know what you can do [eventually]."

Do pitchers relax once the season is over, or do they work on their game?

Many of them go back to basics or work on a new pitch during the off-season. Scott Scudder said he once worked on a flaw in his mechanics right after the season ended. "That was the first thing I concentrated on in the gym during the winter."

*Are rain delays tough on pitchers? Do they ever sit so long
that they aren't put back in a game?*

Yes, delays can be tough. Sometimes a pitcher will be
gliding along pitching a fine game, and then his team goes
on a scoring binge. The pitcher winds up sitting so long
that when he reenters the game he's either tight, or just not
right—not the same as he had been.

Jim Brower once waited one hour and 50 minutes yet
showed no signs that he was the worse for it. He later said,
"The longest I've ever gone during a rain delay [before
this] is about 45 minutes in Triple A. . . . I just went down
to the batting cage every 20 minutes and threw into the
net. Actually, I felt better the second time I went out," he
said. [*Plain Dealer*, 9/25/00]

*What do pitchers think when they go through a period of
getting little or no run support from their teammates?*

In 1991 Charles Nagy got 33 starts. In 20 of those outings he received three runs or less of offensive support.
Nagy said, "You can't worry about it when you go out there.
It can actually make a better pitcher out of you. You get to
know how to pitch in adverse conditions." He said his
coaches told him to do his job and not let it bother him.
"It's a character builder."

*What makes a good home-plate umpire as far as players
are concerned?*

"Umpires today have few guidelines," said Bob Feller.
"Their strike zone is what they decide it is. Sometimes it's

as if the factors for determining strikes include what time of day it is, how many people are on base, what town you're in, who the hitter is, who the pitcher is, what the score is, what time your dinner date is, and what time the plane is going to leave. A great umpire is someone whom the hitter and pitcher can depend on for consistency." [*Bob Feller's Little Black Book*]

How do pitchers adjust to different umpires' strike zones?

Jesse Orosco said, "I know I've thrown pitches where I thought they were strikes, but **I know if I go out there and start arguing I'm going to get away from my game**. So I've got to respect what an umpire is doing.

"All umpires are different—some have a low strike zone, some are high. I watch games for the first few innings on TV [at the ballpark] to see what the strike zone looks like so I know what it'll be like during the game. So when I go out there I'm prepared. If [the strike zone] is the opposite of what I saw, I might say, 'Hey, what's going on?'"

Is there one emotional trait that is particularly valuable to pitchers?

Bob Feller said it "doesn't hurt for a pitcher to have a mean streak in him or at least an attitude that sometimes borders on defiance. It may sound melodramatic, like a line from a B movie, but it's true that **the hitter is up there trying to take bread out of your mouth so he'll have some for his**. You sim-

ply can't let him do that to you, and to your teammates."
[*Now Pitching, Bob Feller*]

How does a pitcher feel when a no-hitter is broken up?

Bartolo Colon lost a no-hitter bid against the Yankees with one out in the eighth inning, on a clean single by Luis Polonia. Colon simply said, "I felt bad about him getting the hit. **It felt like I got punched in the chest**, but I know he's got to do his job, just like I've got to do my job." [*Plain Dealer, 9/19/00*]

Did pitchers from previous years feel they had the right to brush batters off the plate?

Definitely. Tight pitches were called "a little chin music" by Mudcat Grant. Bert Blyleven, who was an Indian from 1981 to 1985, had a flair for humor even when making a serious point, saying, "I've never played with a pitcher who tried to hit a batter in the head. Most pitchers are like me. If I'm going to hit somebody, I'm going to aim for the bigger parts."

Do hitters give more respect to those who aren't afraid to throw inside?

Paul Shuey said, "To an extent. A guy can gain some respect by showing that he does throw inside occasionally, but it's a different thing when you're throwing at heads. **You can get the same effect by throwing at somebody's knees, where they've got a shot at getting out of the way. When**

you throw at somebody's head, you could really kill somebody. That's not really what you want to do. It's going to happen; I mean, I'll throw at somebody once in a while by accident, but when you're doing it intentionally, and for a purpose, for me it's better to just go hard in by the hip area."

Do some pitchers really pitch better when they're a little tired?

Mel Harder said about Bob Lemon, "Lem had one of the best sinkers I've ever seen, but the stronger he was, and the harder he threw, the less the ball would sink. It took him a while to realize that, but once he did, he became a great pitcher." [*Tribe Memories*]

Is there an advantage to throwing submarine style?

"Sure," said Steve Reed. "It's a normal arm motion. It places less strain on the shoulder than a three-quarters delivery." With so many pitchers coming up with arm injuries, submariners deserve a close look. Reed said, **"Submarine pitchers can give you an inning or two 70 times a year**." And that is very valuable in these days of thin bull pens. [*Baseball Digest*, 11/00]

Can a pitcher lose his control and be wild while issuing an intentional walk?

"Some guys have trouble intentionally walking people," said Sandy Alomar. On August 8, 2000, Jason Bere's first pitch of an intentional walk went well over Alomar's head, to the backstop, allowing the Rangers to score a gift run.

"I guess the ball must have slipped out of his hand," said Alomar. [*Plain Dealer*, 8/9/00]

Does a pitcher throw differently for a pitchout?

"You throw a normal pitch [a fastball with the usual delivery] to the plate," said Rick Sutcliffe. "You glance at the runner with peripheral vision, but you do not hold him less closely."

He said what a pitcher will do differently is he won't throw over to the first baseman in obvious attempts to hold the runner. So, keep the runner to his normal lead, but try not to make pickoff throws when the pitchout is on.

Will a pitcher who is getting shelled absorb the punishment to his ego and his earned run average by staying in the game if his team's bullpen needs a rest?

Relief pitcher Paul Shuey said, "You're expected to do that. It doesn't matter who you are. They may protect some people, but **when they're protecting people it's more like a big star who might be a little more fragile and he's going to be a lot better if his confidence is high**. They know if his confidence gets down, he's not going to be as good, so I think there's some protection that way; but for the most part, it's a business and the guys are going to use you to the [advantage] of their business. If that means suck it up—105 pitches in three innings—then that's what you're going to do."

Are some pitchers "big game pitchers," the kind of pitcher who will win in the clutch?

"A lot of guys can win, but can't win 1–0 games," said Bob Feller.

If a pitcher has one overpowering pitch, should he stick with that one most of the time?

Sam McDowell once said, "**It's no fun throwing fastballs to guys who can't hit them**. The real challenge is getting them out on stuff they can hit."

[*Baseball's Greatest Quotations*]

STARTING PITCHING

Do starting pitchers mind when they have to work on only three days' rest?

Most pitchers today would rather not do it. There are, of course, exceptions. Down the tense home stretch of the 2000 season, Chuck Finley won his last two starts in enormously vital games with three days' rest. "It's all mental," he said. "I guess the fourth day just gives you more time to worry."

Satchel Paige said in 1934, "I sure get laughs when I see in the papers where some major league pitcher says he gets a sore arm because he's overworked, and he pitches every four days. Man, that'd be a vacation for me." He said he once pitched in 165 games in a row during his barnstorming days. He joked that that was when "I began to learn to pitch by the hour." [*Baseball for the Love of It*]

*Why is it important to have the starting pitcher work at
least six innings?*

Some Indians pitchers feel that if they give their team a
solid six innings, they have done one of the most important
jobs they have: to eat up innings. Jason Bere said, "There is
more than one way to win a game. My philosophy has always been to try and keep the game close because we have
too good of an offense. I had to stay out there and battle to
chew up some innings."

Managers, coaches, and teammates appreciate it when a
pitcher struggles but manages to spare the bullpen. Bere
said, "This team is going to battle, and as the starting
pitcher I just can't give in. . . . **My job is to keep
the game in striking distance.**" [*Plain Dealer*,
9/6/00]

*Can a pitching coach tell from the starting pitcher's
warmup in the bullpen prior to the game if he has good
stuff that day?*

Not always. On August 8, 1991, Charles Nagy had what
his bullpen catcher that night called "very close to Charlie's
worst stuff of the year." Pitching Coach Rick Adair agreed:
"We're in deep trouble," he said. "Charlie's got nothing."
Nagy, who admitted he couldn't throw a strike while warming up, then came within a scratch infield hit of throwing a
no-hitter. [*Baseball Digest*, 12/92]

How long does it take to get a starting pitcher warmed up and ready to pitch in a game?

Bull-pen coach Luis Isaac said, "I catch all the starting pitchers on the day they warm up. Starting pitchers usually throw between 60 and 90 pitches when they are warming up." However, he added, "**Each pitcher has a different routine**." In 1999 he said the lowest number of warm-up pitches needed by Indians starters was around 68 by Jaret Wright. The highest was Dave Burba's 85 or so.

[*The Morning Journal* c. 5/00]

RELIEF PITCHING

What do successful closers have in common?

Coach Mark Wiley said, "**All the good closers are strike-throwers**." That was the case with Jose Mesa, prompting Wiley to say, "The hitters knew they had to swing or they'd be down 0-1. He made them commit."

[*Baseball Digest*, 6/96]

What do Indian pitchers do in the bullpen to pass time?

"They told lots, and lots, and lots of stories," said Keith Myers, a longtime grounds crew member who worked in the bullpen. "Stories about almost everything but baseball—fishing, hunting, cars, trucks, and whatever went on in their daily lives. They were paying attention to the game, it wasn't like they were goofing off. Then **in about the fifth or sixth inning they'd start getting a little more serious**. The phone would ring, and guys would start getting up—that was their part of the game."

How does a pitcher approach relieving differently from starting?

"When I go nine or more innin's I don't try to strike out nobody," said Satchel Paige. "Just give 'em all a piece of the ball so they pop up on the first or second pitch. No walks. No use wastin' time. But **when I go in for relief, that's different. Then I go in for strike-outs**." [*Pitchin' Man*]

How long does it take to get a reliever warmed up?

"They usually have to be able to get ready in about 20 warm-up pitches," said Luis Isaac. "If they are not in the game after that, I'll tell them to slow down and watch the game a little between throws. **You don't want them throwing so many pitches in the bullpen that they don't have anything left when they get into the game**." [*The Lorain Morning Journal*, c. 5/00]

PITCHES

How does a pitcher go about learning a new pitch?

Cameron Cairncross, the first Australian-born player to wear a Cleveland Indians uniform, said, "You just ask the other blokes how to throw it, how they hold it, how to let go of the ball, what sort of rotation you're looking for depending on the pitch, and you just go from there. You experiment—maybe change your arm angle a little bit or try to get a different spin on the ball. You just gotta play around until you master one thing." Pitchers even vary the amount of pressure they apply to the ball.

How can a pitcher get the ball to move in various ways and directions?

Cairncross said a pitcher will explore different ways to hold the ball with the seams, "depending on what you're looking for. If you're looking for a two-seam, you might want to put pressure on the in [index] finger, off-center the ball, or try no seams. A different arm angle, again, that might help. Turning the ball over might help you too."

Do pitchers often experiment with new pitches during the season?

Pitching coach Dick Pole said, "We do it in the off-season rather than spring training. Get it started in the winter throwing program."

How long does it take for a pitcher to learn a new pitch?

"It's not something you can pick up in a week," said Cameron Cairncross. "It might take you a month or two to pick it up, but you can do it with just a little bit of help from guys on the side—just playing catch."

The next step is for a pitcher to work with a coach. Cairncross said, "You show the coach and see what he says about the ball—if it's worthwhile, and going to be a quality pitch."

At times it's a tedious process. He said, "You might throw

two good ones out of 30 throws, and it's back to the drawing board again—playing catch and experimenting once more." Eventually, the decision might be made to scrap the pitch.

Is it hard to learn a new pitch?

"Not when you're 1–6," said Gaylord Perry. "I learned it [his controversial splitter/spitter/greaseball/whatever] from Lindy McDaniel, but I learned it from watching, not talking to him about it." On the brink of possible demotion to the minors, and sporting a record that was five games below .500, Perry said he grasped the pitch with relative ease.

Which pitch is hardest to teach to a pitcher? Which is the easiest?

"You can't teach somebody to throw a fastball," said Bob Feller. "It's like trying to teach somebody how to grow hair on a bald head. It can't be done. . . . **The curveball, on the other hand, is a pitch that can be taught to most everybody**." [*Bob Feller's Little Black Book*]

What pitch is easiest on the arm?

By far, the knuckleball. "**I never went on the disabled list, never had a sore arm**," said Hoyt Wilhelm. The fact that he threw a "soft knuckleball with a three-quarters delivery" helped him last 21 years in the majors. He pitched until he was 49. [*Baseball Digest*, 11/90]

Why don't more pitchers throw the knuckleball, then?

"It's a tough pitch to master," said Travis Fryman. "The old adage is: 'There's nothing that goes further than a knuckle that doesn't knuckle.' I think that scares some people away from trying." He added, "It certainly has some downsides as far as wild pitches and inconsistency. It's difficult not only for a catcher to catch, but also for an umpire to see effectively. And weather conditions have a tremendous impact upon the effectiveness of the knuckleball as well. Not everyone's willing to take that chance."

Interestingly, Fryman said that unlike many hitters, he doesn't detest the pitch, although he concedes that the slow pitch can throw off a hitter's timing. "Personally I've had a fair amount of success against knuckleball guys in my career, but they can usually mess you up for a couple of days, too."

A few pitchers (Gaylord Perry, for one) had a reputation for using an illegal pitch. Do many pitchers try "doctoring" the ball?

"Hell, everybody who ever pitched has tried to throw a spitter," said Gene Bearden. [*The Boys of Summer 1948*]

"I ain't never thrown an illegal pitch," said Satchel Paige. "The trouble is, once in a while I tosses one that ain't been seen by this generation." [*Washington Post*, 6/10/82]

Is a slow pitch always easier to hit than a fast one?

Not if it's a carefully concealed change-up, as Chan Perry

learned at the hands of Doug Jones. "I never thought I'd strike out on a major league pitch going 58 miles per hour that wasn't a knuckleball."

MANAGING

What's one certainty about managing in the big leagues?
   "If you're looking for job security, drive a mail truck," said Alvin Dark. "Managers always get fired." [*Baseball Quotations*]

Who fires the manager?
   "I hire the manager, but the fans fire him," said former Indians owner Alva Bradley. [*Tribe Memories*]

For players who want to become managers, does it matter what position they played?
   It doesn't have to, but many experts feel catchers make the best managers. Al Lopez said, "One of the main things that helped me later on as a manager is that as a player I was a catcher. I was also captain on most of the teams I played on. I think catchers should make good managers because they are the ones who direct the whole game. Everything is right there in front of them." [*Baseball Digest*, 2/88]

Do managers fear making bold moves?
   Sometimes. But Mike Hargrove said, "That's what they

hire you for." He said it does no good to "cover your butt all day long if your heart tells you a certain strategy is correct."

Does it help a player to have played under many different managers if he plans on pursuing a career as a big league manager?

It can't hurt. Being exposed to different managerial styles and philosophies gives a potential manager a broad background. Lopez said that he benefited from having played under numerous managers. And, he added, "all six of them are in the Hall of Fame." The managers are Wilbert Robinson, Max Carey, Casey Stengel, Bill McKechnie, Frankie Frisch, and Lou Boudreau. "I learned something from all of these men. And when I became a manager myself, it helped me quite a bit to have played for them," he said. [*Baseball Digest*, 2/88]

What's the secret to being a successful manager?

Lopez believed it was gaining control of a team, having solid discipline like a veteran schoolteacher. "**You have to respect the players**," he said, "**and the players have to respect you**."

He felt the most difficult part of discipline was dealing with the bench players. A manager must keep them in a "good frame of mind," according to Lopez.

"The next most important thing is how you handle the pitching staff," said Lopez. "You have to do it right. I was very fortunate. I had two great pitching coaches in Mel

Harder at Cleveland and Ray Beres at Chicago." [*Baseball Digest*, 2/88]

   Ken Aspromonte, skipper from 1972 to 1974, agreed that "the biggest thing in managing a major league team is to establish some sort of authority without making it smothering discipline." [*Baseball Quotations*]

Why is the squeeze play is used less often these days?

   "**The suicide's not dead**," said Mike Hargrove, "**but the American League does play for the big inning** because the ball clubs are built for that. I mean, you've got the extra hitter in there, and usually your DH is a guy that can drive the ball, a high average hitter, or an RBI guy—a run producer. So that's conducive to big innings. You're really kinda cutting your nose off to spite your face if you play for one run all the time. You've got hitters throughout your lineup, so you put the ball in play." He also said he doesn't like the squeeze play since it's "a real chancy play."

What are the right circumstances for the squeeze play?

   Hargrove was asked if he considered putting the play on in a situation like this: Lofton on third base with Vizquel at the plate with a 2–0 count. "Sure you would consider it," said Hargrove, "but I think with 2–0 I'd give him one swing. See if he couldn't get a base hit or drive the ball in the outfield. If you got to 2 and 1, yeah, you'd think about a squeeze.

   "It depends on who's pitching for the other team and

what point in the game it is." Plus, he mentioned you must have the right personnel involved. A manager will let a Vizquel bunt, but, as Hargrove said, "It doesn't do you any good to squeeze with a Jim Thome or a David Justice."

What are managers' thoughts on the safety squeeze?

Mike Hargrove said, "The safety squeeze is a tough play—you're willing to take gambles, take risks, but to me the safety squeeze is one of those where you better be really desperate if you're going to use it." One reason is few batters today are highly skilled bunters. And, while Hargrove recalls when such plays were more widespread, he explained, "It was a different game then than it is now."

How do managers use a relief pitcher as a decoy?

Jesse Orosco said, "**I've been used as a decoy a lot of times** so the other team won't bring up a left-hander to the plate. I may not even be throwing hard [in the bullpen], but just for them to see a reliever warming up. . . . It happens every once in awhile. As a manager, you have to have some tricks up your sleeve."

Is the pressure on the manager greater on the field or off the field?

"Actually, **the easiest part of managing in the big leagues is running the game for nine innings on the field**, when your only thoughts are winning, and how to do it—not what to say in front of a camera before and after the game is played," said

Lou Boudreau. And that's saying a lot, because during his Cleveland career he was not only managing but *playing* during most of those innings. [*Covering All the Bases*]

What's the hardest part of managing on the field, then?

Boudreau said, "I found that handling pitchers—the good, the mediocre, and the not-even-mediocre—was the most difficult part of my job as manager. . . . When to change a pitcher, or stick with him in a jam, was the toughest decision. . . . I was not a good handler of pitchers my first couple of years but soon came to the conclusion that **it's better to replace a pitcher than to leave him in a game too long."** [*Covering All the Bases*]

What's it like being a manager after having been a player?

"I liked managing immediately," said Mike Hargrove. "There is a lot to be said for being the 'yeller' instead of the 'yellee.' Like anyone else, I like the feeling of power. I also like the responsibility. **I get a bigger kick out of watching my team perform well and knowing I had a hand in it than I ever did even in my best days as a player."** [*The Curse of Rocky Colavito*]

How do the players make managing in the majors different from managing in the minors?

"On a minor league team," said Mike Hargrove, "the managers can say, 'Fellows, this is the way it's going to be done, and if you don't like it, we'll find someone else to take your place and you can go home.' You can't do that with Albert Belle. You can't tell that to Carlos Baerga, Dennis Martinez, Kenny Lofton, or Eddie Murray. There are no other people to take their places, and they know it." [*Burying the Curse*]

COACHING

How do you coach pitchers at the major league level?

Ray Miller said, **"If the talent's not there, there's nothing you can do**." And, "If you have to teach pitches at the major league level, you're not going to win." Beyond that, he said, there are three keys to pitching: work fast so hitters are kept off balance; change pitches so the batter can't time a given speed or recognize a pattern; and throw strikes to keep in command of the game. After all, he said, pitching is nothing more than "an elevated game of catch." [*Baseball Digest*, 9/90]

Is it possible to over-coach a player?

Ray Mack once complained that his hitting suffered from over-coaching. "I always believed I could hit, but the way it worked out, **I let too many people try to tell me what to do, and I tried too many different things**. I would have been better off if I'd gone on my own." [*Tribe Memories*]

Sam McDowell said his pitching suffered, early on, from the same problem. "I had very low self-esteem as a young pitcher. . . . I had no idea how to pitch," he said. "With Cleveland, [manager] Birdie Tebbetts called every one of my pitches. I mean every single pitch. I wasn't learning anything by him doing that because he never sat down with me after games or between innings to tell me why he wanted me to pitch a certain way. Really, I didn't have to take responsibility for how I pitched. If I lost, I could always just blame Birdie Tebbetts." [*The Curse of Rocky Colavito*]

BENCH JOCKEYS AND HECKLERS

Do players still "bench jockey"—yell things at opponents to rattle them?

Pitcher Justin Speier said, "There are certain people who joke around with each other, but [as for] getting on opponents? Not really, most guys are professional. There are a lot of guys, with free agency, who have played with a lot of guys on other teams, so there's a certain professionalism.

"You go out and you want to get the best of them that day and then that's it. **There's not too much razzing**," said Speier. Most bantering back and forth is just lighthearted teasing and good-natured joking.

How do players feel about getting booed?

Bill Selby said, "Sure, it hurts. We all have hearts and feelings, too," he said. "It would just be like me going to somebody's job and heckling them—telling them they suck and 'You're the worst.' It's part of being a professional athlete to learn how to tune that out."

How do players feel about hecklers and foul-mouthed fans?

When Pedro Martinez complained about some obnoxious Cleveland fans, Sandy Alomar countered, "When you go to Boston, it isn't easy either. Sports is like that wherever you go. That stuff doesn't matter. I don't really care."

However, he added that fans can go too far, as in cases where they toss around racial comments or make threats. "But you're going to run into people like that anywhere you go, not just in Cleveland. Don't penalize everyone because one person said it; they're just idiots." [*Elyria Chronicle Telegram,* 9/15/00]

Do players on the field pay attention to what fans are yelling from the stands?

Some do, some don't—or at least they claim not to. **"You really don't pay attention to the crowd**," said Richie Sexson. "That's something I learned in Cleveland, where the fans aren't very knowledgeable. You can go 2-for-2 and then strike out the third time and get booed off the field." [*Plain Dealer,* 8/27/00]

But the otherwise extraordinarily affable Jim "Mudcat" Grant once said, **"Those fans say things about your mother that make you want to get up in the stands and punch a few of them."** [*Joy in Mudville*]

In basketball, Michael Jordan was known for wanting the ball on crucial plays. Do baseball players feel the same way in the field?

Rick Manning certainly did—especially during Len Barker's perfect game. "I wanted that ball to be hit to me," said Manning. "I was begging for it, especially when Lenny needed one more out. I knew if it was hit anywhere close to me, I'd get it." [*The Curse of Rocky Colavito*]

THE BALLPARK

Does the condition of their stadium matter much to players?

When Municipal Stadium started to decay, few players enjoyed working there. Richie Scheinblum said, "The only good thing about playing in Cleveland is you don't have to make road trips there." [*Baseball's Greatest Quotations*]

"In the middle of a game, a guy from another team would ask me how I could stand to play there for eighty-one games a year," said Andre Thornton. "They didn't see the Stadium as major league. It was demeaning, at best a slight step above Class AAA." [*The Curse of Rocky Colavito*]

Doug Jones said, "It's a museum," he said. "A museum of unnatural history."

As a player, Mike Hargrove didn't like Cleveland's stadium either. He once said, "There's nothing wrong with the stadium that a case of dynamite wouldn't cure."

MISCELLANEOUS

Do players mind switching positions?

"It wouldn't be my first choice, but if it's good for the team, then fine," said Jim Thome, who made a much-publicized move from third base to first base. [*Tribe Memories*]

Jim "Mudcat" Grant was glad to change positions when he was a spring-training prospect, because it got him a job. As he recounted it later, "[Coach] Red Ruffing told me that they were going to let me go, but if I went to the manager and told him that I could pitch, they might let me stay around a little longer. So I said I was a pitcher. I wanted to do anything to make it." [*The Curse of Rocky Colavito*]

Do players think it's ethical to steal the other team's catcher's signs?

The Indians of 1948 are now known to have been stealing catchers' signs throughout their championship season. Two players from that team had slightly contradictory opinions when asked about it later.

"If I was on the other team and pitching against the Indians, yeah, sure I'd resent them stealing our catcher's signs," said pitcher Gene Bearden. "But like everybody said, **other teams were doing it, so we might as well, too.**"

Third baseman Al Rosen said, "That stuff has been going on since the game began and, while I can accept a coach or a base runner doing it, I can't condone it being done with a telescope or television camera or anything of that nature. **To me that's as unsportsmanlike as anything I can think of.**" [*The Boys of Summer 1948*]

Off the Field

THE CLUBHOUSE

If a team calls up a slew of players on September 1, when it is legal to expand a team's roster, does the locker room ever run out of lockers?

"I haven't seen that yet," said Cameron Cairncross, who spent September of the 2000 season in a very crowded clubhouse. "This place is huge." Even with televisions, tables, and chairs everywhere, he said there was ample room. He joked that a player "could hide in the back [of the facilities at Jacobs] and no one will see you."

Do players have to tip the clubhouse workers for all the services they provide both at home and on the road?

"No question," said Bill Selby. "In the lower minor leagues it's a lot different. **There's no question a lot of your money goes to tips, but that's all part of the business end of baseball**. They take care of you; you take care of them. That's the way the cycle works," he said.

*Is there a certain amount a player must pay, or is it more
like when a restaurant patron leaves a tip for the waiter?*

Selby said he believes the clubhouse workers see it as an
issue of "Pay me what you feel like I'm worth. If I do the job
for you, then compensate me." He added, "Rookies are not
expected to pay as much as guys who make more money,
that's an understood rule. If I go to a clubhouse and I'm a
rookie, but the guy washes my clothes—say I bring some
extra laundry, and he takes care of me, sure, I'll give him
more than what I'm supposed to."

What do players do to kill time in the clubhouse?

Many players use free time to read, answer fan mail,
grab a snack or drink, do puzzles, discuss their fantasy
football league, talk with friends, grant interviews, sign
several dozen baseballs for charities and other causes.

Even though players get to the park hours prior to game
time (a major leaguer typically spends around seven or
more hours a day at the park), there isn't an overabun-
dance of free time. Often they have to get taped, stretch,
get loose, hit in the cages, go over the opponents, and, in
general, prepare for that day's game.

The Indians of 1995 loved cards and music. Carlos
Baerga played the card game Spades, while Albert Belle
said he preferred "Pluck and Boo-ray, a Cajun card game.
Also, Paul Sorrento and I had a Sega Genesis, and we
played hockey and Evander Holyfield boxing." Not much
has changed, except perhaps the card game and the video
systems, which, of course, are far more advanced now than
back then.

Julian Tavarez watched cartoons. "*Scooby Doo* is my favorite." he said. "It's funny. Time goes by fast when you turn on cartoons." [*Plain Dealer*, 8/00]

Other popular television shows over the years have included wrestling, action movies, the Olympics, tons of ESPN shows, and fishing shows. Believe it or not, at one time a huge clubhouse hit was *Lifestyles of the Rich and Famous*.

Some players even go to chapel for religious services. When he was with Cleveland, Belle stopped a rare interview with a writer, excusing himself so he could attend such a service prior to a Sunday-afternoon contest.

Many players from the past complain that today's players clear out the clubhouse as soon as they can after a game. They say that in their time they'd stick around, talking over the day's game, learning from each other. Is this criticism valid?

No, according to Sam McDowell. "Old-timers say over and over that players nowadays don't talk baseball. What they really mean is [talking baseball after a game] in a bar.

"Modern players don't want to sit around a bar. They're more into conditioning; more sophisticated about health. They talk over breakfast, lunch, or dinner.

"In the past players *would* talk about the game. You'd have six, seven guys who'd love to sit around two, three hours after the game. They'd be talking, but while drinking free beers in the locker [room]. The only other place available to them were bars after games."

What else do players do in the clubhouse after a game?

Albert Belle said, "I tend to stay after a game and maybe watch videos of opposing pitchers [for the next, upcoming game], or watch my at bats."

What's the food like in big league clubhouses?

"You get two or three different main course meals," said Selby. "It's just like eating in a nice restaurant, but it's convenient. After B.P. you can get drinks. Sometimes guys will order in—Chinese, Japanese, something like that. When they do, the attendants get the food and bring it to the players."

Do players pay close attention to what they eat?

Most players today do. "Generally I keep a pretty good diet to try and be in top condition for peak performance," said Albert Belle. (His body fat was under 10 percent at the time.)

C. C. Sabathia said, "Last season, before I started eating healthy, on the days I was pitching I always went to Wendy's and got a Big Bacon Classic and supersize fries. Now that I've stopped eating fast food, I don't know what I'm going to do this year. I'll have to find something new, maybe a sandwich from Subway." [*The Sporting News*, 3/19/01]

HOME AND FAMILY

Do wives consider their lives to be glamorous?

That may not be the right word, said Jackie Nagy, but "It

is definitely a unique experience, and I'm fortunate enough to have had a lot of years at it. It was a little bit harder on [Charles] in the beginning—he was newly married, on the road a lot, getting adjusted to just not having a regular schedule.

"There are perks beyond a doubt of what he does, but there are drawbacks sometimes that I think people tend to overlook. They sometimes forget that these guys are people. The poor guy still has to take out the garbage and change the toilet paper."

What's a typical day like in the life of a player and his wife when the Indians are home?

Andrea Thome said, "Usually we go to bed pretty late, so we get up fairly late, too, around 10:00. I'll get up and make him breakfast, but he's a pretty good breakfast maker himself. Then we just putter around the house—that's our time to enjoy each other because that's really it for our time alone.

"Once we get dressed and leave the house, sometimes we'll go to lunch or we'll run errands we need to do. We try to do that together; we don't always get to, but, again, when he goes to the park at 1:00 or 2:00, I don't see him again until midnight," she said.

How can a player's long absences affect his relationship with his young children?

Annie Waits, wife of pitcher Rick Waits, said, "Rick shares my distaste for single parenting, [for] the kids often having no father. He misses out on the everyday communication that makes my children so close. **My kids actually prefer me when asked to make a choice, and this must sadden their dad**, although we both realize the favoritism is due to my proximity." [*Safe at Home*]

When a player is traded, does it affect the families of other players, too?

It sure does. Jim Thome, for example, was upset when his good friend Richie Sexson was traded. Andrea Thome said, "It's really hard on us. I still keep in touch a lot with Kerry [Sexson's wife]. Jim and I were in their wedding . . . so we are very close with them."

Do players discuss games with their family when they get home?

Some do; some don't. Jim Thome, for one, talks things over with his wife. She said, "We sit down every night and watch Baseball Tonight. It's a staple in this house, and sometimes in the morning we've got to watch it twice. We talk about [the games], and he likes it that I like to talk about it.

"There are nights when I know, if he maybe strikes out three or four times or something, **I'm not going to say, 'Well, why didn't you swing at that pitch?' I would never do that because I'm not his coach**," she said.

She and her husband will talk about items such as "Boy, did Pettitte look tough tonight," or "Was his curve sharp tonight," and other inside baseball topics.

Do husbands explain facets of the game to their wives?

"For sure," said Jackie Nagy, "we talk about a lot of elements of the game. Things that are working for him at the time, things that aren't working for him. He'll wake up one morning and say, 'Hey, have you seen my curveball? I lost it last night.'

She said, "I've never really questioned him about, 'Hey, why did you throw a 3-2 pitch inside or a fastball up and in,' I don't follow the game well enough to ask him those specific points.

"Some plays I don't understand, like we saw a catcher's balk recently, and in all my life I've never seen a catcher's balk. So we definitely talked about that, and he explained it to me."

She said she feels she has learned a lot of baseball over the years "through osmosis."

What are the drawbacks to being the wife of a major league player?

Vickie Bannister, Alan's wife, said, "Alan's [been] unable to be with me at both of our babies' births." She felt especially bad for him.

For Gloria Bell the worst thing was "being alone at first, then having so many responsibilities alone." Toby Harrah's spouse Jan singled out "the constant relocating; saying good-bye to dear friends." Finally, Annie Waits had a litany of items, including watching Rick suffer through a frustrating 2–13 season, and sometimes having to listen to a losing game on the radio. That bothered her because she couldn't be there "to help and [would have been] unable to do so even if I was there." [*Safe at Home*]

How do players react to slumps at home? Can it affect their home lives?

Prolonged slumps can take their toll, and some players are real bears as they hibernate through a slump. Shortly after her husband suffered through a terrible slump in September of 2000, Andrea Thome said, "I try not to address it. I just will say to him, 'Hey, do you want me to make you a lucky egg sandwich?' And he'll say, 'Yeah.'

"Finally, toward the end of this one, I said, 'How are you feeling?' And he said, 'Well, I'm either too fast or I'm too slow, but, you know what, it's part of [playing the game] and I'm going to figure it out. And it's going to correct and it's going to be over.' And it sure was," she pointed out, as Jim blasted some important home runs down the final stretch of that season.

Do wives go to every game?

"Well, I'm guaranteed to be there every fifth day," laughed Jackie Nagy, referring to the fact that her husband, Charles, works only when his turn in the pitching rotation comes up. "Now that we have a three-year-old, I don't go to as many games. Early on in his career I was there every night. We usually just pick two nights a week now and take our daughter down—it's kind of a long night for her."

What does a wife think when she sees her husband in an on-field brawl?

"I really don't worry when I see that kind of stuff because I know in baseball it's what I call pretend fighting," said Andrea Thome. "**They never really do throw punches**. Even when Jim charged Rheal Cormier in 1999, I happened to be on that trip, and I was like, 'I can't believe that's my husband down there'—like the gentle giant. But he didn't give it his all, and Rheal kind of moved and Jim kind of flipped over and I knew he was OK.

"But that evening the Cormiers gave us a ride home from the ballpark in their car. Their two kids were in the back, and we were all just telling jokes. [Fights] are just part of baseball; it's nothing personal."

Do the players' families socialize with the manager's family?

Jackie Nagy said the Indians management is very family friendly. "The two managers I've known have families that are a very integral part of the team. The wives sit with the team. On some teams there's not a lot of mingling; with the Indians there is, and it's fantastic. There's not a differentiation between the two different levels. "

INJURIES

How does a wife react when her husband gets hit by a pitch while she's watching the game?

Wives may understand that it's all part of the game, but it still tends to bother them. Andrea Thome said when Jim is hit by a pitch she "can see by his body language if it's serious."

However, when he broke a bone in his right hand, she said, "he didn't really give a good indication that it hurt as bad as it did when it happened. But he called me after that game at Tampa Bay and said, 'Well, guess what?' And I was kind of waiting, and I knew when the phone rang—I just had a feeling [it was rather serious]. Injuries are *no* fun," she concluded.

Do players expect other players to play despite being ill or slightly injured?

In spring 2000, David Justice missed four games in March with a strained quadriceps. One Indian grumbled, **"If I'd have missed four days it would have been headlines. That guy misses four days and no one writes a thing**. This guy is making $7 million a year, and he doesn't want to play. Last September we had guys playing hurt every game, but this guy didn't want to play." [*Plain Dealer*, 10/27/00]

Justin Speier said, "Oh, yeah, definitely. I mean, you see guys that go out there, real professional about it. They go out there and play with little, nagging injuries—no one's ever 100 percent. Guys who play through that show us younger guys that 'Hey, you go out there and you play through aches and pains like that.'

"My dad [major league shortstop Chris] played 100 percent maybe three times in his whole career, and he played 19 years. That's just one of those things, you're not always going to be [fully healthy], you've just got to give it 100 percent," said Speier.

THE FRONT OFFICE

Should a baseball team be run differently from any other business?

Bill Veeck didn't think so. "**A baseball team is a commercial venture, operating for a profit**," he said. "The idea that you don't have to package your product as attractively as General Motors packages its product, and hustle your product the way General Motors hustles its product, is baseball's most pernicious enemy."

[*Veeck as in Wreck*]

What is a real baseball promotion?

Veeck defined a promotion quite simply. He said, "Anything you do to enhance sales is a promotion." Even if his team weren't a pennant winner, Veeck would proclaim proudly, "We can't always guarantee the ball game is going to be good; but we can guarantee the fan will have fun."

[*Veeck as in Wreck*]

His longtime helper Rudie Schaffer agreed, and scoffed at what passes for a promotion today. He said, **"They give away a bat or ball, and it's called a promotion. To me that's not a promotion, it's a giveaway**. A promotion is something you generate out of thin air and make fly."

Should the general manager worry about what fans will think about trades?

John Hart said, "Controversial moves? I hate to make them. But I do because the hat on my desk says general manager. **I can't be best friend; I can't be super fan. I am general manager**." [*Cleveland Magazine*, 3/01]

What strategy does the front office use when drafting amateur players?

Dan O'Brien, who has been a scouting director and once served as the Indians' Senior Vice President for Baseball Administration and Player Relations, said there are two ways of drafting: "You can draft by position or draft the best athlete available regardless of who's playing that athlete's position at the major league level and at the other levels. **We go after the best player all the time**."

Is there a preferred schedule for moving a player up from the minor leagues to the majors?

O'Brien said, "It's in the best interest of the player not to put him on a timetable [as some teams do]. People progress at their own rate. The important thing is getting to the finish line—the majors—not how fast you get there. We don't want to be quick in our judgment."

Do long-term contracts lead players to become complacent?

Lou Boudreau observed, "The players get multiyear contracts and high salaries. They have security, which has to change their perspective. In my day, a two-year contract was a rarity."

He added, "I'm not saying players shouldn't get as much as the owners are willing to pay. But I think that, with salaries as high as they are, it changes the attitude of the ball players." [*The Boys of the Summer of '48*]

As Rick Waits put it, "**It used to be you got paid after you did it. Now you get paid before you do it**."

For Carlos Baerga, a long-term contract wasn't just about money. "All you have to think about is baseball. You don't have to worry about having to put up numbers or having to do this or that. When you go out there it's not for money—it's to win a ring." [*Baseball Digest*, 7/94]

Besides financial stability, what reasons do players have for signing a long-term contract?

"Six years feels like a long time to be on a team, but I was really looking for a family and a home," said Omar Vizquel [*Tribe Memories*]

*Are older players jealous of the huge salaries and attractive
contracts of today's players?*

Some are, of course. Larry Doby, though, said, "I kinda
look at it from the standpoint of earning power, which lasts
a very short time for players. Time changes things. When I
broke in I got the minimum, $5,000. Whatever they're get-
ting now, fine."

In all honesty, he admitted he would love to play baseball
nowadays. "Sure," he said. "Who wouldn't want to be a mil-
lionaire? You'd be lying if you said no."

He also said he believes sky-high salaries "will not ruin
the game. If the owners didn't have the money," he said
with a deep laugh, "they wouldn't pay it."

Bob Feller said, "They are entitled to it, and I am all for
it. In fact, it is a changing world for the old-timers, too. I
make more money now traveling around the country and
appearing at card shows with hobby groups than I ever
made as a player."

TRADES

*Do some general managers trade a player simply because
he did something that made the front office angry?*

This has happened throughout the history of baseball. At
times a manager may request that the team dump a player.
However, Al Rosen, a former Indian and later a general
manager, said, "**I was taught long ago, by
Gabe Paul, to never get mad at a player
and deal him**." He felt such a hasty decision can

backfire. He often chose to protect what he called his "assets" and to build his players up. [*Baseball Digest*, 4/92]

Do managers ever feel bad about losing a player?

When the Indians and Sandy Alomar parted company, Charlie Manuel said, "Sandy is like a son to me. He's been a credit to our organization, without a doubt. This was a contract thing more than anything. We had to make sure we had a catcher. If Sandy [as a free agent after the season] signed with another team, we would have been left without a catcher, and they're hard to find." [*Plain Dealer*, 11/18/00]

How do players feel about being traded? Are they businesslike and realistic, knowing trades are part of the game, or does the human side of baseball surface?

On one level players of course understand trades are inevitable, but they also admit that, as human beings, it truly hurts to get traded.

Glenallen Hill said, "**My reaction on being traded? Do you want to watch a 235-pound man cry?**" [*Plain Dealer* c. July 2000]

After being traded from Cleveland to the Yankees, David Justice said the trade "turned my world upside down." He added, "I absolutely did not expect it. I don't think there was anyone that expected it." Still, he said he realized that "money was an issue." He also, like all players, knew that the bottom line is this: baseball is a business. [*Elyria Chronicle Telegram*, 9/16/00]

Sometimes the change helps a career. Dave Otto left an

Oakland team that was a perennial contender and came to the Indians in 1991, yet he said he was not disappointed. "I'm finally getting a chance here to pitch. It's good to get a change of scenery."

When Kenny Lofton was traded to the Atlanta Braves, he said to a *USA Today* reporter, "I've done everything they've asked me to do in Cleveland, and I thought I would be rewarded. I guess they rewarded me by trading me."

The man who went along with Lofton to Atlanta in that swap was Alan Embree. When he read that the Braves would free up a whole lot of salary by dumping David Justice's $6.2 million off onto Cleveland, Embree's take on the trade was to quip, "I figured I was the point-two."

Bob Wickman, when he came to the Indians, said, "I had four great years with the Brewers. It was wonderful. Leaving the Brewers' organization is not what hurt. Baseball is a business, and everyone knows that. What hurt is having to leave the family members I had in the area." [*Plain Dealer*, 8/13/00]

Sometimes, for a relatively unknown player, being part of a trade can almost be a claim to fame. Steve Demeter said about being traded for Norm Cash, "To be considered on par with him at one time is kind of an honor." [*Tribe Memories*]

How does a player feel when he plays against the team he formerly played for?

Juan Gonzalez had an off year with the Tigers in 2000. When he first faced them as an Indian the following year, he was booed resoundingly. He said, "I have no enemies in Detroit. The way I played there last year, I would have booed myself."

Most players, though, want to excel against their former team. In his first six games against Detroit, he hit .320 with two homers and seven RBI. [*The Lorain Morning Journal*, 4/23/01 and *USA Today Baseball Weekly*, 4/18-24/01]

FREE AGENCY

How does a front office decide how much to offer a free-agent player?

"Bidding for free agents is always a crap shoot," said general manager Phil Seghi after signing Wayne Garland during the first year of free agency. "No one is worth $2 million. We simply tried to gauge what Garland's value to the club might be." The temptation to steal a 20-game winner was palpable, even though Garland's won-loss record was 7-11 for his career prior to his 20-victory season of 1976.

Garland himself said he wasn't worth the amount Cleveland dished out. **"No one is worth that much. But if the Indians were willing to pay it, I was willing to take it. Who wouldn't?"** Of course, his average salary of $230,000 a year totals only 15 percent more than what a rookie making the minimum salary got for the 2000 season. [*Tribe Memories*]

What do older players think about free agency?

"The players, because of free agency, are seeking contracts for more money than any of us old-timers ever dreamed of getting," Bob Feller observed.

It's only natural, though, said Feller, as "the market for star players available as free agents is fantastic. The owners want star-quality players even though they may not come to them to stay, but to help them win ball games and maybe a pennant and a shot at a World Championship." Some free agents are like security guards at events—a.k.a. a Rent-a-Cop; perhaps a comparison to a soldier of fortune is more appropriate. In any event, some of those star free agents last only a year or so with a team, but owners are willing to roll the dice with high-profile free agents at times.

How have players' agents changed the way players relate to their team?

Lou Boudreau said, "To me, there's also the question of loyalty, the way things are today with agents being so prominent, and so important. **Instead of a player owing his total allegiance to his team, his manager, and his teammates, it seems that too many are loyal primarily to their agent**, the guy who got them their big contract, and will be negotiating their next contract." [*The Boys of the Summer of '48*]

How about other former players, what are their thoughts about the days of negotiating on their own versus using agents?

Naturally men like Rocky Colavito would have loved to

have the leverage of free agency at negotiating time. "We had to fight for every dime we got. There were no agents, and I wasn't the type to toot my own horn. The only time I'd get mad and get my 'Italian' up was when they'd say you didn't do this or didn't do that. They wanted you to be loyal to them, but they were not loyal to you."

Other thoughts on players' agents?

Dave Garcia, manager of the Indians from 1979 to 1982, was pointedly sarcastic when speaking of agents. In 1981, when Cleveland posted a record of one game above .500, he said, **"If everyone contributes what their agents say they'll contribute, we'll have 172 wins and no losses in 162 games**."

THE MEDIA

How important is it for a player to have good relations with the news media?

Some players think the news media are irrelevant. **"I don't worry about that stuff**," said Manny Ramirez. And that's not simply a modern attitude. Back in the 1940s, pitcher Don Mossi earned the nickname 'The Sphinx' for being silent and inscrutable. "I came here to pitch, not to talk," he said. [*Tribe Memories*]

Bob Feller, though, thought it was important to talk to reporters. But it wasn't always easy to do. "When you make a bad pitch and the hitter puts it out of the park and you cost your team the game, it's a real test of your maturity to be able to stand in front of your locker fifteen minutes later and admit it to the world," said Feller. "How many people in other professions would be willing to have their job performances evaluated that way, in front of millions, every afternoon at five o'clock?" [*Now Pitching, Bob Feller*]

Do players read their own press clippings—are they curious about what the print media has to say about them?

Many players grab one of the national publications that are strewn throughout the clubhouse, but a few say they won't or don't read the local papers. Albert Belle, not surprisingly, had strong feelings on this topic. "**My preference**," he said rather emphatically, "**is to *not* read the local paper**. I usually don't. They tend to be more negative." Belle said he would read *USA Today* "now and then."

Sam McDowell said, "In the old days every player read everything [on the sports pages]. We might have said, 'I don't care, I don't read them [bad press clippings],' but we did. Today when some players say they don't read the garbage, they don't."

FANS

Are the fans ever rude when players are out in public? Do they ever, for example, pester players when they eat out?

Andrea Thome said, "No, and Jim will always sign. Normally people will wait till they see that we've finished eating. If somebody does come up [before then], Jim will always just say, 'Would you mind waiting until after?' And I really can't think of a case where anyone's been nasty about it. Usually they understand. Sometimes they might say, 'But I'm leaving now.' Jim will say he's sorry, but he's got a sandwich with Thousand Island dressing dripping out of his hand, what can he do?

"But most of the time people are just really, really wonderful here. They seem to love him in Cleveland."

What do wives think about rude fans at the ballparks? How does it affect them, and what can they do about those pseudo-fans?

Sharon Hargrove wrote, **"The saddest part is watching the foul comments hurting your kids. That's their daddy who is taking the heat. It breaks my heart**. One time I remember a fan really being on Mike's case in Cleveland and [their daughter] Kim just looking back at the guy, turning around, staring at Mike on first base, and just letting the tears come."

Patty Blyleven, Bert's wife, once confronted a heckler, telling him to shut up or get out of the park. When he said he had paid his eight dollars and was entitled to express his thoughts, Patty "took out her billfold, wrote out a check for eight bucks, gave it to the guy, and requested he go elsewhere and try something else that would be more enjoyable." [*Safe at Home*]

"You try to ignore them to the best of your ability," said

Jackie Nagy. "We [wives] are a little bit isolated, we're in a family section, but you can still hear the boos. I would say the fans are terrific, but they are very quick to boo," she said with an understanding smile. "Everybody's going to have a bad day. I understand when you pay what you pay to see a game, you want to see a good game. Sometimes my heart just bleeds for some of these guys who get the quick boo."

How faithful and loyal are former players?

Some, like Bob Feller and Rocky Colavito are, in their minds, forever tied to the Indians. Despite having problems with Cleveland's front office at times, in 1992 Colavito, looking back over his career in Cleveland, said, "I love the city. The fans are fantastic. My rapport with the fans was always wonderful."

AUTOGRAPHS

How is a star like Thome able to take care of myriad autograph requests?

Andrea Thome said, "That's part of his going in early—sitting down to sign. I don't know how much he gets, but it's stacks of mail and he tries to get through a lot of it." In addition, he's good about signing as he strolls around near the dugouts.

Did any Indians collect cards when they were kids?

Sure. Carlos Baerga said, "When I was a little kid, I always collected baseball cards, but I never took them to get them signed by anybody." He did, however, enjoy the bubble gum that came with Topps cards. He also said his hero was fellow Puerto Rican Roberto Clemente.

He believes autograph seeking started getting big in the 1980s when "everybody in Puerto Rico started going to the ballpark for autographs. Now all the kids bring cards for everybody to sign. I sign for everybody."

What do big league players like Baerga think of the autograph craze?

"It's crazy," Baerga said, pointing out that fans bring virtually every item imaginable to be autographed. "Whatever you have [that's connected with] baseball, they bring it— batting gloves, everything."

Although the mania was inexplicable to the All Star second sacker, he said, **"It's nice to sign autographs, to take care of the people. This is a show we put on, and they pay for it. Why not take care of them?"**

Any interesting childhood stories from an Indian involving autographs?

Charles Nagy tells of the time when he was around five years old and lived in the same apartment building as Tom Seaver. "I used to bother him for his autograph every day," he said. "He hated me."

What about players' connections with autograph shows?

The old joke about Bob Feller and his propensity for

signing tons of baseballs goes like this: The rarest baseball of all is one *not* signed by Feller. Even he said if there's a fan somewhere in the world without his autograph, he must not have wanted it.

He is one of the first players ever to take part in card shows, charging money for his signature. "I doubt if I was the first big [star] to go to a card show and be paid, but I was one of them. I've done a lot of shows," he said.

During those shows, how many times does a player like Feller put down his John Hancock?

He said he might sign between 700 and 800 autographs in three hours, and he's been doing that now for four decades.

Do players have a policy about when or where they'll sign, or for whom?

Most Indians will sign, at least from time to time, at the park. Five-time strikeout king Sam McDowell, who's long retired, said he won't sign for adults if he suspects they may be card shop owners or collectors asking for his signature simply so they can sell it.

"If there was a way of proving the autograph was for a kid, all players would sign, no problem. I'm guessing 90 percent of the people are selling the autographs. This leads to cynicism by players.

"A kid came up to a player in Toronto and let the cat out of the bag, thanking the player for his vacation. The player had signed seven or eight autographs for the kid over the years, and the father sold them," said McDowell, describing one profiteering family.

Why do people crave a signature so much?

Feller theorized, "It might be a little bit of an ego thing. Sometimes I wonder myself." Many feel that fans want something to authenticate the fact that they had a brush with a star. They can take, say, an autographed ball home to show friends and proudly display the ball for future bragging rights.

Are players and former players who charge for their autographs being mercenary?

Feller said, "I've heard people say that; it doesn't bother me at all. In public I sign for free, almost everywhere I go—at fantasy camps, in restaurants, in hotel lobbies, on airplanes, and at the airports. I furnish a lot of balls and pictures and sign them for charities to auction off."

Is part of the business marketing yourself?

Feller thinks so. "**It's to the player's benefit to be personable**," he said. And while younger players, men still in their prime, can get away with not beaming a Hollywood smile when they sign, later they may regret not marketing themselves. Feller said, "When [your] career is over and [you're] looking for a job—you may be in your 40s and you still got a lot of years to live yet, and you want to do something because you can't [just sit and] look at

those old clippings, it's to your advantage to have good
media relations and also have a good public image." So, he
said, making friends, having a skill (even one like doing autograph shows), and developing a positive image (for example, signing for kids and doing charity work) can really
help a former player.

*Do the Indians still take part in an off-season speaking
circuit to stir up interest in baseball?*

The Indians still take part in this annual event. Matt
Underwood said, "There are two weeks between the AFC
Championship and the Super Bowl, so the Indians are
going to do it the week before Super Bowl, what they call a
'dead week.' We'll be out and we will literally canvass the
entire state. It starts in Cleveland, then we usually go to
Columbus. From there, there are stops in Mansfield, one in
Norwalk, Walnut Creek, Youngstown; we went to Erie,
Pennsylvania, last year.

"Some of the visits are overnight trips. For most you're
just on the bus—you hit maybe two stops then come home.
You do a lunch and a dinner, then come home that night,"
he said.

TRAVEL

*Do some players like the actual travel—being on a bus,
train, or plane?*

Not so much now, but Rocky Colavito said that during
his playing days, 1955–1968, there was a great deal of loy-

alty and friendship among the players, and one reason was the way they traveled. "The camaraderie in those days was outstanding. I'm not saying everyone [always] got along with everyone, but for the most part they did. When I first started, we rode trains together and got to know each other. It was a nice feeling."

Is there a team rule—like those of some other big league teams—about how many times a wife may travel on the road with her husband?

"No, they have the unspoken rule where **you probably don't want to be going on every single road trip or they start to call you 'luggage,'**" said Andrea Thome, laughing. "The other guys joke around and say, 'Does your wife need a team bag?' and that kind of stuff." Such teasing is enough to get the unwritten rule across.

As for Andrea Thome, she plans her trips "around if I have friends in certain cities, [plus] there are certain cities I love to go to, like Seattle and New York. I know there are places, too, where Jim likes to go and hang out with the guys. Like he loves Kansas City, because of the river boats there. And I get a feel [for it by] talking to him. 'Hey, this trip coming up, what do you think?' and he'll say, 'Yeah, come.' Or he'll say, 'Well, I was going to do this.' That's just how we do it."

Andrea Thome also said some Indians wives in the past have had nannies "just so they could spend time with their husbands occasionally on the road."

Do the Indians own their own plane?

Paul Shuey said, "We do not. I think there might be a few teams that do have their own charter plane, but most of the teams that I've heard about charter flights." That helps a great deal on, say, getaway days when a game might go into extra innings. Instead of having to book a new flight on the spot, as was once the case, the traveling secretary knows the charter is waiting for the team.

Bob Dolgan wrote in the *Plain Dealer* that these planes "have about 100 seats. That gives the players plenty of room to stretch out, about one row per player." That sure beats the long, arduous train rides spanning the country from Boston to St. Louis in the days before flight in the world of baseball.

Do wives go along on the charter flights?

"Oh, no," said Andrea Thome, "we fly separately except for when we have a family trip, and we didn't have a family trip this year [2000]. I don't know if that was because of the changing of the guard—it was Charlie's first year, settling in. It was probably a decision that [needed to] have been made early in the season, but early in the season this year it was a little dicey with the losses and with Charlie's [poor] health. The trip just didn't come up. Typically we have one family trip a year." Usually, she said, Mike Seghi, team travel director, gets the ball rolling in picking the trip for families to tag along on.

When players are on the road, can they leave free tickets for friends and family?

"We're allotted six tickets for every game we go to. If it gets to where I need your tickets, then I borrow them," said Bill Selby, referring to how a player might need more than six tickets if the team is visiting a city where he has a lot of family living nearby. For example, when he goes to Texas and is near many of his relatives, he borrows more tickets. In other cities he probably gives up some or all of his "comps."

Another scenario: "Say a visiting team comes here and we're full up every night, they can't get enough tickets, so they have to buy tickets to get in." Usually the home team will be able to drum up extra tickets for a player, but the money comes out of his own pocket.

Do players prepare differently for games when they are on the road?

Albert Belle said, "When we're on the road some of us do come in for early defense or early hitting. Usually for a 7:30 game I get there around 5:00. I get there and get settled in. I get early stretching, hitting, and treatment. After a game I tend to stay and lift weights."

Cairncross said that if he's expected to be stretching at 4:30, "I'm usually here around 1:30, 2:00. I like to get here early, get dressed, and relax—sit around, have a drink of water, and take it all in."

On the road he gets to the park around the same time so he can "watch a bit of telly [television]. I get a bite to eat, replenish my water, do a couple of weights, strap it on, and get going." Most guys, he says, come to the park earlier when they're on the road because **"you get sick of lying in your bed, so you might as well go to the field**. But it's a good time to catch up on your rest, too, on the road."

Is staying at the park late while on the road normal?

No, actually that's unusual. Albert Belle, however, would sometimes stick around for hours after games. But, he said, "In certain situations I get out fast, like in Texas and Seattle because I've got relatives or friends I played ball with there. So after a game I hurry to get out and see my relatives and go out to dinner and catch up from the last visit."

SPRING TRAINING

What goes through the mind of a rookie during his first spring training?

A young Ray Fosse said, "When I went to spring training, I was scared and nervous, trying to live up to all the things I read that people were saying about me. I guess I tried too hard, got into a real rut and then couldn't get straightened out," he said. [*The Sporting News*, 5/16/70]

What can really help a young player gain confidence?

Graig Nettles said that when he came to the Indians from the Minnesota Twins as a young man, he had two goals: "To prove I can hit lefties as well as righties, and to show that I'm a better infielder than some people seem to think."

He was able to achieve those goals early in his career, and two things helped. First, Alvin Dark, his manager during his first year in Cleveland, showed confidence in him. Nettles said, "When I got here and Alvin said he was going to stick with me no matter what happened, I stopped fighting the ball so much, and now I'm able to relax and play what I think is my normal game. Because I'm relaxed, I'm more fluid instead of being so rigid, and that's very important."

Secondly, Indians coach Kirby Farrell worked Nettles hard. "I hit him ground balls for almost an hour straight . . . we're trying to work him so hard that everything becomes mechanical and automatic," said Farrell. By the end of his first spring training with the Indians, it was estimated that Nettles took about 20,000 ground balls. [*The Sporting News*, 3/28/70]

ATTITUDE

During the long years of losing in Cleveland, did players develop a negative attitude?

Many did, yes. Lou Camilli, an infielder back in 1972, said, "They ought to change our name to the Cleveland Light Company. We don't have anything but utilitymen."

Four years later when Cleveland's second baseman Jack Brohamer was traded to the Chicago White Sox, he was elated. "I'm not sure how much I'll play," he said, "but if I have to sit, I'd rather sit in Chicago than Cleveland." [*Baseball Quotations*]

When the Indians were suffering through losing season after losing season, was there anything to be proud of?

Sam McDowell, who managed to win 20 games for a poor Indians team, told *Baseball Digest*, **"I'm proud of the work I did on a team that should never have been close to the top**. We didn't have the talent other teams did. Yet, when we came to play, they respected us. Sonny Siebert, Luis Tiant, and myself. They knew they were in for a battle. We knew we'd finish sixth or seventh when we left spring training, but dammit, you were going to have to beat us." [*Baseball Digest*, 4/83]

How do players feel about showing up other players? For example, if a pitcher whiffs a batter and then puts on a dramatic display, does the batter ignore it or does it bother him?

It's only human nature for one player to resent another trying to gloat. Jesse Orosco said, "You don't want to see that happen, and it really doesn't happen much. I mean sometimes you see somebody standing there watching a home run for awhile and that's not fun for a pitcher to see. **It's not good for a pitcher to scream at the batter after he struck him out or do arm motions**. I come from the old school: hit the ball, run, throw, catch it—that's the way the game should be played."

Orosco continued, "Look at Carlos Perez. He's very animated, but not many players say anything because he started that way. Rickey Henderson's the same way. That's up to individuals if they enjoy it or not. I mean I look at Kirby Puckett. As soon as he would make contact, even if he hit the ball 400 feet, he was already at second base by the time that ball landed because he hustled all the time. Never showed anybody up, and it was just refreshing to see a player like that."

Do players openly declare they're shooting for a personal record?

In 1970, coming off a 304-strikeout season, "Sudden" Sam McDowell announced he wanted to become the top strikeout artist of all time. "**Sure, I want to be number one—number one in all of baseball. What's wrong with that**? Records are important to me, especially now. I've reached a certain level so that pride is a factor, too." [*Sporting News*, 2/14/70]

Do players crave attention and recognition?

Even players who aren't stars have their own goals and desires. Scott Scudder said, "Everybody wants to be seen and noticed, 'Hey, this guy's a good player.' I just want to be consistent, that's how I'll assert myself." He added, "**It sounds weak, but if I can give six-seven innings, and give my team a chance to win, I'm doing my job.**"

*Do players really care about trophies such as the one
presented for the Rookie of the Year Award?*

When Kenny Lofton lost the Rookie of the Year to Pat
Listach of the Milwaukee Brewers, Clevelanders felt it was
a joke. Lofton said, "I'm not going to dwell on that. I
thought either I would win and the voting would be close,
or that he would win big. It turned out he won big." It also
turned out Listach was a flash in the pan, while Lofton was
the real deal.

*Ken Griffey, Jr., once said it's impossible for a player to
hustle all the time during the long season. Would all
players agree?*

Travis Fryman said, "I disagree a little bit. I think you
play hard all the time. I think probably what Ken is sug-
gesting is it's really not possible to go 110 percent, to use
that adage, all the time. You play at a very high level—what
percentage, I don't know. You're hustling all the time, but
you're not going wide open all the time because you can't
physically do that on a daily basis."

By way of contrast he pointed to football, where "you
hype up for six days to elevate yourself emotionally and
physically to play one game. Baseball, we play every day for
such a long period of time—it requires a certain mentality
of pacing yourself. So **you play at an elevated
level, but it's not wide open every day.
It's just not possible to do that**."   •

Can an entire team take on an attitude that translates into victories on the field?

Lou Boudreau said one of the biggest reasons the Indians enjoyed their great 1948 season was their positive attitude. "We were like a bunch of college athletes, all together on the same page, and everybody knew what had to be done when he was called upon." [*The Boys of the Summer of '48*]

Are ballplayers as confident and self-assured as they appear to be on television, at the park, and during interviews? Or, like the rest of us, do they have some insecurities and anxieties? If so, is this especially true of players in the minors?

Players are human beings, and, as such, they all have their problems. Sam McDowell said, **"Most players have low self-esteem. They've been taught since they were seven years old that they're important *if* they're winning**. [A player] gets this from parents, from Little League, and from high school coaches."

Sharon Hargrove concurs that players' egos can be delicate. She said, "Their ego is only as big or as little as the success or failure they had in their last game or season." [*Safe at Home*]

Meanwhile, Paul Shuey phrased his thoughts in a rather philosophical way, "You can't fear failure and you can't fear success." [*Plain Dealer*, 9/21/00]

Do players get spoiled by the special treatment they receive?

Sharon Hargrove wrote, "**It is hard for these guys to grow up because everything is done for them**. On road trips they have a schedule that tells them when to arrive at the airport—what airline, gate, and time. They are—literally—handed their boarding passes. They don't see their luggage again until they are at the hotel and it is brought up to their rooms." [*Safe at Home*]

PENNANT FEVER

When their team is in the middle of a pennant race, do players indulge in "scoreboard watching" or do they just concentrate on their own game?

In late 2000, as the Indians were clinging to a lead in the race for a wild card berth, Jim Thome said, "We've tried not to scoreboard watch, but it's tough not to. You look to see what Boston and Oakland are doing. But, at the same time, you have to take care of your own business." [*Elyria Chronicle Telegram*, 9/12/00]

Sandy Alomar said, "I don't care about that. I try to put together a good at bat. **We have no control over [other teams' scores], so why put extra pressure on yourself.** You've got to stay on yourself every play." [*Plain Dealer*, 9/23/00]

How do players handle the pressure of a pennant race?

Omar Vizquel, who liked to spend time in his basement playing his drums or listening to music, said, "You just

want to go to a place where no one's around. Just get to another atmosphere, another mindset."

Dave Burba said he refused to watch the other playoff
contenders on TV. "Why? Does it matter? I can't control
what the other team does. I'm certainly not going to spend
valuable time watching another baseball game."

In contrast, Steve Karsay said, "I can't go by [the TV]
without taking a peek." [*Plain Dealer*, 9/30/00]

What does it feel like to win the World Series?

"A player's—and a manager's—first World Series is like a
child's first taste of ice cream. It's never enough," said Lou
Boudreau. [*Covering All the Bases*]

DISCIPLINARY ACTION

*Do players worry much about fines and suspensions doled
out by their leagues, or are they so wealthy they think petty
fines are a joke?*

John Smiley, a onetime 20-game winner, said, "I think
they're pretty fair; they're not as bad as the NBA. Some of
those $10,000 fines in the NBA are pretty steep. To take a
guy out of the lineup for three or four days, or for a pitcher
to miss a couple starts, that's [a] pretty high [penalty].
And if the team doesn't pay [a player's monetary fine], like
the year Marge Schott, the Reds owner, didn't pay, the guys
have to pay out of their own pocket and that's a lot of
money for some guys."

What are the longest suspensions usually for?

Jesse Orosco said, "They make it the stiffest fine they can [for fighting] because they're trying to eliminate these things from happening.

"If you give guys just one day or two days [suspensions] or you don't fine them, stuff could happen again and trigger [more on-the-field problems]," said Orosco.

In August of 1999, after getting plunked by a pitch, David Justice not only charged the mound against Troy Percival of the Angels, he also threw his batting helmet at Percival.

Both combatants were issued a three-game suspension. While such a suspension is normal for an assault on the mound, throwing equipment could have stiffened the suspension. Manager Mike Hargrove of the Indians admitted, "I'm surprised it's only three, and very thankful."

Justice concurred, "I thought it would be a lot worse. I would prefer it be nothing, but I realize there's got to be some penalty. Three games is not bad." [*Plain Dealer*]

Do suspensions affect all players equally?

Orosco pointed out that if a relief pitcher and a starting pitcher are suspended for, say, three days each "it will hurt the reliever more." But he said that it's unavoidable. "What are you going to do—you going to suspend a starter for 21 days? You could say he has to miss two starts, but you can't do that either because then you ruin the whole team because of the rotation [being out of sync]."

THE "GOOD OLD DAYS"

Do players typically feel that the time period they played in was the best?

That's usually the way it works. Take Rocky Colavito, for example: "I always deemed it an honor to have played major league baseball, especially in my era. I'll take that era. We had so many stars then. It was a golden era, I think," concluded the man known as the "Rock" long before pro wrestling's WWF bombarded the airwaves.

Are players today more greedy and jaded than the old-timers were?

No, says Herb Score. **"Society has changed, but the players haven't. . . . Younger players act tough, but inside they're excited."** He also said that what makes it seem like there's a vast difference between the players of the 1950s and those of nowadays is "the exposure to the media"— that is to say, if a player did something illegal, controversial, or outrageous back then, the media wouldn't play it up so big; they might have even covered it up. Now every move by every player is analyzed, exposed, and broadcast coast to coast.

Score said, "A competitor is a competitor—forget salary. When a player crosses those lines, he's not thinking about money; he wants to do his best."

Sam McDowell said, "Today many players are sophisticated. They read sports psychology books and books on nutrition. There are higher levels of education among the players now."

RETIREMENT

How does it feel to end a long career?

Dennis Eckersley summed up his emotions upon retiring by saying what is typical of many players, "It's hard to walk away. Baseball has been a major part of my life since I was eight years old." [Russell Schneider]

What are some baseball wives' thoughts on the end of their husbands' careers on the field?

Cindy Pagel, Karl's wife, said her husband's release was the hardest thing she ever had to cope with. Sharon Hargrove, in her book *Safe at Home*, tells of how Cindy "knew, after the long years in the minors, that he no longer had the desire to play. He was ready to hang 'em up. It was hard for her not to pressure him. She loved the baseball life, but she loves Karl more."

In her book Hargrove described the point when a player is turned loose for good: "**When it ends, it ends. All of a sudden you are on your own—no teammates—and you must start over, in a hometown where you've lost touch**. It was all there for the asking while you were playing. Now it's a new direction without direction—scary." [*Safe at Home*]

How do players react when inducted into the Hall of Fame?

While the usual reaction to a Cooperstown induction is elation, Lou Boudreau said in his Cooperstown speech, "I'm really humbled by this because I never considered myself a superstar like Williams, DiMaggio, or Aaron." Of course, that didn't deter him from being ecstatic, too.

[*Baseball's Greatest Quotations*]

Gaylord Perry said, "**it's a great honor because it's recognition by peers**." The fact that guys he knew well such as Willie Mays and Willie McCovey were enshrined there made induction into the hall even more special for Perry. He called his induction the number one highlight of his long career.

Do all players miss the game after their playing days are over?

"I played baseball from the time I was big enough to walk, but now that I'm out of the game, I don't miss it a bit," said Ray Murray. "I did at first, but I got over it in a hurry, put it out of mind. I forgot it. The only thing I ever missed was the guys." [*The Boys of Summer 1948*]

SCOUTING

Do major league scouts sometimes rely on their gut instincts?

Yes. Cy Slapnicka, the Cleveland superscout who unearthed Bob Feller, will never forget the day he saw the 16-year-old Feller back in 1935. "He was pitching on the outskirts of Des Moines [Iowa]," said Slapnicka. "I watched a couple of pitches from the first base line, and I got the funny feeling that this was something extra.

"So I moved over behind the backstop and sat down on a car bumper. It must have been a hell of an uncomfortable seat, but I never noticed it. All I knew was that there was a kid I had to get. I didn't know then that he was smart and had the heart of a lion, but I knew I was looking at an arm the like of which you see only once in a lifetime," he said, almost in awe. [*Baseball Digest*, 12/92]

Can a diamond in the rough be detected, scouted, and then, most importantly, succeed at the big league level?

It happens fairly often. Kenny Lofton had little baseball experience prior to being drafted. He had only played baseball in college because, he said, "I just wanted to see where I stood." After being a four-year starter in high school, he didn't play again until his junior year at Arizona.

Even so, the scouts saw him and recognized that, as Lofton said, "I had some tools," so they drafted him. He was the 17th-round pick in the June 1988 draft. They loved his speed, and before long he was in a minor—then a major— league uniform. [*Elyria Chronicle Telegram*, 3/8/92]

Why are there so few submarine pitchers in the majors? Does it have anything to do with scouting?

Steve Reed, who throws from down under, said, "One of the big problems is that submariners don't light up the radar guns—and **so many scouts are locked**

into the radar gun these days." If a pitcher doesn't throw hard, sometimes he doesn't get a second look. [*Baseball Digest*, 10/00]

ANNOUNCERS

Are announcers journalists?

No, said Pete Franklin. "**The announcer is an extension of the team's public relations department**. . . If it's raining, he tells you not to fear, because the weather will clear. In fact, this rain delay is a blessing in disguise because it gives you more time to get down to the ballpark and buy tickets and hot dogs." [*You Could Argue But You'd Be Wrong*]

Who do the announcers work for—the team's front office or the station?

Matt Underwood said, "The Indians took the [radio] rights in-house beginning with the 1994 season when they moved into Jacobs Field. TV is separate; those people are signed by Fox and Channel 43."

How does a broadcast announcer prepare for the game?

For a home game at the ballpark, Matt Underwood's day begins sometime between 3:00 and 3:30. "The first thing you usually do is go in the clubhouse to talk to some of the players—usually you have an idea of who you want to talk to. Maybe it's the guy who did something unique in the game before or had the big hit or a good pitching performance. Maybe you talk to someone to check on an injury, see how they're feeling.

"Usually sometime before the game I check with the manager to see what's going through his mind—if he has any changes he's going to employ in the game, maybe a change in the lineup," he said.

Frequently he'll ask the manager a question about the previous game, such as "Why did you bunt or hit and run in a certain situation?" This helps Underwood get a feel for how the manager is running his game so he can pass such information on to his audience.

Describing the routine for a 7:05 game, he said, "Around 4:30 we start taping the pregame show when it's a home game and it's on Fox. We usually finish taping around 5:00. Sometimes I have to do a radio interview as well, so I'll seek out a guy I want to interview, waiting until he's done with his batting practice. Then you grab him and talk to him for two to three minutes for the radio pregame show."

He's done on the field by 5:30, and it's time to head up to the booth to fill out his scorecard. He likes to "jot down a lot of statistical notes and numbers that you want to have at the ready. By the time that's done and you grab a bite to eat, it's 6:30, and that's when we go on the air for the pregame show."

After the game it's time for the postgame wrap-up show before finally hitting the road to "head on home."

What's so hard about doing the preparation?

Underwood said that facet of his job makes him feel like

a student doing his homework. It's difficult at times, as well as being time consuming, to "compile stories, anecdotes, and statistics."

He went into more depth, saying, "If you want to get technical, **the hardest part of the job is timing**. While Tom [Hamilton], Mike [Hegan], and I had worked together in the past on pregame shows, it's different when you're in there together [the booth] during the game. Timing is critical. Chemistry is critical, and that's something that takes a little while.

"I think we assimilated as a group very quickly, and that was something that was one of my goals—to make sure that I didn't always sound like the new guy."

Who trains announcers such as Underwood, helping them learn what to do for a pregame routine and so on?

"I basically broke in under Nev Chandler. I learned a lot of the mechanics, the fundamentals, from Nev. I learned a lot from Tom Hamilton just in my first year [2000]."

Underwood said he observed "little things—things that maybe the audience would never even think about, like scorecards. How exactly do you make a scorecard, and what's the ideal scorecard in terms of statistical information that you can jam into it?"

He gave another illustration. "Here's a little thing I learned from Tom, a little thing that means a lot to a broadcaster. When he fills out his scorecard, if he's got a switch hitter in there, he uses a different color ink for the first name and the last name. That way when he looks down, he realizes that's a switch hitter."

Underwood expanded upon that idea. "I write down all the right-handed hitters in blue ink, all the left-handed hitters in red ink. It really helps you with the visiting club, and you do that with the pitchers, too," he said.

What should an announcer do when he makes a mistake?

"When I misspeak," said Herb Score, "I know it right away, and I correct it. Once it is out of my mouth, it is gone. You can't change it. Just don't try to cover up your mistakes. **You're on the air for three hours a night and saying who knows how many words. You're human. You'll make mistakes**." [*The Curse of Rocky Colavito*]

Is there a difference between doing play-by-play and color commentary?

"The rules are different," said Matt Underwood. "When you're the play-by-play, you're essentially directing the game from a broadcasting perspective. As an analyst, it's your job to answer when the play-by-play guy either asks you for a thought or he pauses. Then you've got to get your thought in and get back out so he can continue the broadcast." This calls for speed and for the ability to be concise. It's also part of the timing element he feels is so vital.

As he put it, "You can't be lingering with your thoughts or struggling to get a point out because **while baseball is a slow game, you'd be amazed at**

**how quick it is when you're up there try-
ing to get a thought out in between
pitches**."

*Broadcasters try not to interrupt each other. How do they
avoid it?*

"It's just like batting practice," said Underwood, "you just
do it over and over again and eventually you get it."

*How do the announcers communicate in the booth without
fans overhearing their conversations?*

Announcers have a control known as the "cough switch"
that, when pressed, kills their microphones so the audience
won't hear noises such as coughs or throat clearing.

Underwood said, "The only time we'd [both hit those
switches] is if , say, you've got a question that you don't
want to ask over the air, so you may hit both cough
switches and say, 'I can't see who's warming up in the
bullpen, can I use your binoculars?'"

*Do radio announcers have a way to speak to their directors
through their microphones?*

Underwood said, "No, that's the difference between radio
and TV. In TV there's a cough switch, and there's a 'talk
back' button. You hit that and your mike is killed over the
air, but it goes directly to the producer or the director in
the truck and you can ask him for a close shot or replay.

"In radio, it's just us. There's an engineer who sits directly behind us, but a lot of times if we need to say some-

thing or ask him something, we'll hit the cough switch and turn around to our engineer and ask things like, 'Do you have that score on the Yankees game?'"

How should a former player use his playing experience when he becomes an announcer?

He shouldn't, according to Bob Neal. Herb Score related the advice Neal gave him when he was a fledgling in the booth: "You're a broadcaster now. Don't live on what you did as a player. **No one cares about when you pitched. Make your reputation as a good broadcaster.**" [*The Curse of Rocky Colavito*]

How far should an announcer go in criticizing players on the field?

"The thing I believe in is that the players are the stars, not the broadcasters," said Herb Score. "I don't try to be an expert on every play."[*The Curse of Rocky Colavito*]

Lou Boudreau, who was a Chicago Cubs broadcaster after his Cleveland playing/managing career, said, "**In the beginning it was difficult for me to refrain from being critical**. It wasn't that I was inclined to second-guess. I'd been second-guessed enough in my 15 years as a major league manager to know how unfair it is to have somebody on your back all the time saying—after the fact–that you should have done something else.

"I was more concerned about a tendency I might have to be critical of a bonehead play. . . . I didn't like dumb players when I was managing, and I knew I wouldn't like dumb players when I was broadcasting." [*Covering All the Bases*]

If a player is closing in on a record during the course of a game, how can an announcer learn what the record is in order to tell the fans who currently holds it, when it was established, and other interesting facts?

They rely on comprehensive notes prepared by the media department. If other data is needed, announcers have tons of record books in the booth. Either the announcer or engineer can look items up.

Underwood said, "If you're doing the color role and you want to know what the record is, one of you goes to the back and gets the book." A quick search usually reveals the information the announcer needs to pass on to the listeners.

What do announcers do during rain delays?

"Normally, we grab a guest," said Underwood. "You look around the booth to see who else is in the press box. . . . We had Jim Kaat on one night, and that was a great conversation we had with him. We had Ray Fosse on one night—he's always enjoyable. You try to get a guest on the air with you.

"When we have Mike Hegan in the booth it makes it easier, too, because you've got three guys who can sit there and talk about what's going on."

Is there much job security in baseball broadcasting?

"Broadcasting is a lot of fun, but it's not like baseball,"

said Mudcat Grant. "You don't control your own destiny. **Ballplayers in the TV booth are like streetcars, you come and go.**"

GROUNDSKEEPING

Does the grounds crew try to give their team a literal home-field advantage?

"This is a game of inches," said Emil Bossard. "**An inch is often the difference between a base hit and an out. We try to have the inches go our way.**" Bossard was a sort of legend. He began work for the Indians in 1935 (with two sons to help him) and lasted until the mid-1970s (with at least one son keeping the dynasty alive until 1985). Some teasingly called Emil "the evil genius of groundskeepers" because of his ability to groom the field to aid the Indians.

He'd slant the foul lines to help Indians bunters, or, if the team lacked bunting skills, he'd slope the lines the other way to hinder opponents' bunts. He would soak the ground in front of home plate if the Indians had a sinker ball pitcher working, or he might pack the dirt tight if the Indians' batters were prone to hitting Baltimore chops for hits. In short, he knew all the tricks of his trade. [*The Cleveland Indians Encyclopedia*]

How are the rules about the height and slope of the pitcher's mound enforced?

Keith Myers, a longtime grounds crew member at

Cleveland Municipal Stadium from 1986 to 1993 for both the Indians and the Browns, said, "Once or twice a year a Major League Baseball roving guy would come in and check to make sure the mound was 10 inches above home plate, and that it sloped one inch for every foot from the pitching rubber all the way to six feet out."

Myers added that, in theory, every mound in the majors should be basically the same, but in reality, they are not. Different pitchers prefer throwing in different parks in part because of their mounds.

What other stadium feature does Major League Baseball measure?

The lights. Myers said an inspector would "put stakes in the ground at different spots all over the field, and he'd test the candlepower to measure each section of the field to meet major league standards [for player visibility]. He went over everything thoroughly."

Does the pitcher's mound need special care?

For seven years Myers took care of the pitcher's mound. "As soon as the game was over," he said, "we would do all the things that were necessary to get the field ready to play because you never knew if it was going to rain all day the next day. You didn't know when you'd next be able to get back on the field.

"During the course of a game the pitcher digs out the area in front of the rubber pretty good, and the landing area [which is also torn up a bit] for either a left- or right-handed pitcher is different—there's one on one side and one on the other. So you'd have to fill those holes in.

"First, you sweep out any loose dirt in those holes. You pour some water into the hole, you sweep out the water, lay some fresh clay on top of that, then you stamp the clay in to maybe a half-inch below the rubber. You try to blend it in so you have a nice slope on the landing area. Then you'd drag the mound and run a broom over it, and it would be ready for play the next day."

Why does the grounds crew replace the bases during the game?

Myers said the bases get a bit scuffed, but not all that dirty. Plus, the bases are touched up with whitewash after each game. So, the change is "more for just looks," he said. Plus, there are enough bases to constantly have a fresh, clean supply. Myers said, "There are four sets of bases—one for batting practice, two 'gamers', and a spare set."

How often is the grass cut?

"You cut every day if you can," said Myers. "Most days when you can cut it and there are no weather problems, like the grass being too wet, you don't pick up the clippings. But if we let it go for a couple of days, you have to have a guy collecting the clippings."

What are the main functions of a grounds worker before the game?

Myers said, "I would drag and retamp a couple of areas

on the mound after batting practice. Every guy had his own responsibility. Two guys would be taking the cages down, you'd have a guy taking each of the nets away, and my responsibility was removing the fungo net in front of home plate on the grass. It's there for when guys hit shots right into the ground—without the net they'd beat the grass to death."

How many workers does it take to keep the field in shape?

Myers said, "We had six full-time guys and about six to eight part-time guys. Two of the full-time guys took care of the infield and another guy did home plate. One man cut the grass and one watered it—he was the one with the most seniority so he got the [most coveted] job. He even had to come in when the Indians were out of town to operate the sprinklers. He had to put the sprinkler head in the ground, turn the water on, and then move the sprinkler head to a different section to be watered. It could be half an hour to an hour per section. That's why the guy could be at the stadium all day." Of course now, in the newer, baseball-only parks, all the watering is done automatically.

What's the biggest challenge for the grounds crew at the major league level?

The worst scenario is when rain hits. Myers said putting out the tarp is, despite appearances, no walk in the park (pun intended). "If you get more than one rain delay in a night, the tarp gets heavier and heavier because it starts getting waterlogged. That would really wear on you, and you're out there getting soaking wet," said Myers. The workers are also fighting the wind, which makes the tarp chore nearly impossible at times.

What's the toughest groundskeeping job?

"**I was the backup grass cutter, and it was one of the hardest things you can ever imagine**," said Myers. He pointed out that to the fans in the stands the striped appearance of the grass after being mowed is aesthetically pleasing, but for a novice it is not easy to achieve. "There are three reels on the mower, and they all come across evenly. After the grass is cut, there are little rollers that push the grass down in one direction causing an illusion—depending on which way you're looking at it. Looking the 'down' way [with the grass looking bent down] the grass seems to be light in color; look at it coming from the other direction and it seems to be a dark stripe. The hard thing to do is keep the lines straight as you cut." On the tractor, with little room for error and, at times, with the sun glaring in one's eyes, this is no routine task.

Does the Cleveland grounds crew have any special "tricks of the trade"?

At the old stadium, the crew had a special (and very quick) way of getting the tarp out, according to Myers. He explained, "Two ropes were rolled into the tarp. The ends of the ropes had a ring on them. We'd bring a tractor out and attach the rings to the back of the tractor, so the tractor would pull the tarp all the way out; we would unfold it.

Each worker ran to his spot, and would grab a fold in the tarp, unfold it, run back to his new spot and unfold the tarp once more. A little tugging would pull the tarp out to its full extension for maximum coverage. Most teams will have the guys behind the tarp pushing it out. They don't use the rope system anymore even at Jacobs Field. We were pretty quick." He estimated that from the moment the umpires told the crew to hustle out onto the diamond, it took two to three minutes to get the field covered.

Aside from the hard work, is there an upside to being on the grounds crew?

Myers said, "Being the sports buff that I am, it was tremendous. I had the time of my life during those eight years that I worked there.

"Being around the athletes was a big part of it, there's just something about it that's hard to describe. We were down by the bullpen most of the time on the visiting side, and guys would try to give our workers the hot foot," he said. The Indians of that time period were "pretty tame," not engaging in many pranks.

UNIFORMS

Who takes care of Cleveland's uniforms—is there a "tailor to the stars"?

It's hardly as glamorous as Hollywood, but Mark Wasie, who runs a laundry service in the Cleveland area, is in charge of the uniforms. While most uniforms are basically the same, Wasie says Kenny Lofton and Wil Cordero want the uniform legs to be tightly tapered. Meanwhile, Steve Karsay and Jim Thome prefer their sleeves be let out as wide as possible. [*Plain Dealer Sunday Magazine*, 10/29/00]

Since uniforms get dirty and acquire rips and holes during any given day, how does the tailor keep up with things?

Wasie told the *Plain Dealer*, "On game nights I have dinner, go to bed, and wait for the phone call." While the uniforms are washed at the ballpark, Wasie can get called in to Jacobs Field for a sewing session as late as 3:00 a.m. Like television's Paladin, Wasie has his tool and he will travel— his portable sewing machine is lugged to Jacobs Field each time he has work to do.

VENDORS

What is the life of a beer vendor like?

In September of 2000, vendor Frank Biggio was featured in an article in the *Plain Dealer*. It told of how he pops open about 170 beers every game, and how he totes two cases of 16-ounce beers up and down the stairs of Jacobs Field, not an easy chore. The 29-year-old graduate student at Case Western Reserve University is not your stereotypical vendor. He said he actually has "been keeping a spreadsheet on my performance this year."

He also said, "We work the same sections all the time." He enjoys that because, he says, "over the course of the season, we have regular customers."

Do vendors use gimmicks to make fans want to buy something from them?

Jim Carle is a vendor at Jacobs Field. Fans who have heard his gravelly voice don't forget him. Instead of handing a bag of peanuts to a fan, he tosses the bag. When the fan catches the bag, Carle shouts out, "Nice catch, sir, and welcome to the Show." A smile spreads over the fan's face, and another Carle sales pitch with positive reinforcement has worked.

He said, "**As I started selling peanuts on the long home stands, my voice got deeper and deeper. The fans seemed to be appeased by the low voice, so I kept it**," he said, not unlike a comedian mentioning he was going to keep a joke in his act.

Do vendors work the entire park?

Carle says no. He, for example, mostly works "from home plate to right field, always the lower deck, but **the slower the peanuts go, the farther I travel**."

Another vendor, Timothy Britton, said the upper deck steps are a lot steeper and a bit more challenging, so usually the younger vendors work the nosebleed areas.

Where do vendors pick up their food and/or drinks?

Britton said, "There are six commissaries strategically located throughout the stadium—three upstairs and three downstairs. The farther away you stray from your assigned commissary, the harder it is because you have farther to travel—more time is involved and so you earn less money."

At the commissary the vendor checks in, gets credit for products sold, then picks up new supplies. Britton added that upon returning to the commissary, "You have to turn in your 'load' money before getting a new 'load.'"

Do vendors always sell the same product all year long?

No. Carle said, "They assign one product per person at the beginning of the year. Usually by the middle of the game when that product gets a little slow, they allow you to switch depending upon seniority or previous day's sales."

Even though beer sales sag during chilly months, those vendors are, according to Carle, "very loyal to their product," perhaps because even on cold days tips can help vendors out. Britton said part of their "fierce loyalty is because they've been glamorized by recent commercials." He also said being a beer vendor is considered to be more macho than selling, say, a lemon drink.

How are the vendors paid?

On a commission basis. Britton said, "Vendors who sell food products get 15 percent plus tips." He said that beer vendors are at one disadvantage—their sales take longer because they have to open and pour each beer. However, beer vendors tend to get more tips than those who sell food.

Even with good pay for many of the days they work, a

second job is necessary for about 80 to 90 percent of the vendors who toil at Jacobs Field.

What kind of pay can vendors make?

It depends on the product sold, but beer vendors' commission is good enough that one vendor said he makes about 50 cents per beer sold. At that rate, a vendor can pocket about $75 to $100 per game—even more with tips. "I'm averaging about 24 cents a beer in tips," said Biggio.

Be aware, though, that it isn't easy money. John Nuttall, the general manager of Sportservice, said, "**People look at beer vendors and don't think much, but these guys make a lot of money *and* work incredibly hard**."

MINOR LEAGUES

What is the biggest difference between the minors and the major leagues?

Bill Selby said, "It's the pressure, especially when you come to a team like this. Look, you're out there every day, you've got to do your job because it's important to win.

"**At the minor league level a lot of times it's develop, get better, and get your at bats. Here it's help the team; you gotta win.**

"You're here, do what you can do and help us out when you're called on, be ready."

On the other hand, in the majors "everything is taken

care of for you—the spreads [of fine food], the travel, everything's a lot easier; this is the pinnacle of baseball. But that's what you work for."

Is it true minor leaguers (especially in the low minors) still eat a lot of cheap food like peanut butter and jelly or lunch meat?

"No question," said Selby, not long removed from such a scenario. "People don't understand. I come from a small town and I'm the only guy from around there that's ever played professional ball. They think just because you're a professional you make a lot of money, and that's not the case. **You live check to check and you work in the off-season when you're in the minor leagues because you just don't make a lot of money**. So, guys do eat a lot of junk in the minor leagues; they just don't have the money."

What are minor league salaries like?

Selby said, "When I first got drafted, I was making $850 a month, and that was for five months. That was it. Don't get me wrong, I love what I do, but it gets tough to make ends meet. If you're married on top of it, it's just really tough."

Do players feel that a call-up to the majors is helpful even if they are sent back to the minors shortly after their big league debut?

Charles Nagy did. He termed his first call-up for a "cup

of coffee" a big help. "I was thrown into the fire, so to
speak," he said. "I had never faced big league hitters before.
Looking back, I was awestruck; it was a big learning experience. **Pitching *is* a learning process. You
learn something new every day about
yourself or the people you face**."

Is life difficult for managers down in the minors, too?
Sure. Joel Skinner, who managed the Indians' Triple-A
team at Buffalo, said, "You have to learn your personnel
and be prepared. **In the minors, you manage
the game while coaching third base**." He
said that one big difference in the big leagues is that the
third base coach gets the signals from the manager, then
relays them to the hitters. [*Plain Dealer*, 11/19/00]

Do many minor leaguers have self-doubts?
Sam McDowell said players in the minor leagues do in-
deed lack security and confidence, more so than major
league players, and that seems quite natural. "In the minors, they still view a request for help as a sign of weak-
ness," explained McDowell.

*How long do players typically have to make the trek from
the minors to the big leagues?*
Jim Lemon, who broke in with the Indians and later was
a minor league hitting instructor, said, "Your life in this
game can be very short. You've got to be prepared to go all
out. If you're not able to convince someone that you can
play a little bit, you'd better be ready to start another voca-

tion." In short, he said, "**When you sign a contract, you have three or four years to learn everything you possibly can and display all the talent you have.**" [*Small Town Heroes*]

How difficult is the transition from high school baseball to playing ball in the minors?

When Richie Sexson was eighteen years old, he was a couple of weeks out of high school, playing ball for the Indians at their Burlington, North Carolina, farm team. His reaction: "This is a long way from home. I've never been to North Carolina before. I went to New York once. But that was with my parents."

He continued, "I can't believe the pitching here. **In high school I never saw anything but a fastball. Here guys throw curveballs. Even with 3-0 counts. They change speeds. This is really something.** In high school I was hitting around .470. I'd settle for half that right now." He was hitting .185 when he spoke those words back in 1993. [*Small Town Heroes*]

How are the minor leagues different from the majors when it comes to promotions?

A. J. Maloney, a mascot for Buffalo, a Cleveland farm team, said, "There's always something going on here." He contrasted minor league conditions to those of a game he had attended at Fenway Park in Boston. He said everything seemed so quiet at the big league game. "It seemed like something was missing," he said. [*Small Town Heroes*]

What could be done to help minor leaguers?

Jim Thome proposed an idea that would at least help many minor league players when their all-too-brief playing days are over. "I'd change the minor league pension and give them more pension for certain years they played in the minor leagues—just like the major leagues. Maybe not [based on] ten years [as it is in the majors], but coordinate it where the minor leaguers would be taken care of."

How would a player sum up his feelings about the minors?

As Scott Scudder once said, "Once you spend time in the minors, you know the majors is the place you want to be, and you want to get there as fast as you can."

What does it feel like to be demoted to the minor leagues?

"**Going back down to the minors is the toughest thing to handle in baseball**," said Gaylord Perry [BaseballAlmanac.com]

ROOKIES

With salaries being what they are today, do younger players ever still have to scrimp?

At times, yes. Andrea Thome said that not only do minor league players have it tough financially, "sometimes even in the majors, these players that are making $225,000 or something like that—that sounds like a great living to a lot of people, but also you need to realize these people have a home in Florida that they're paying on and they also have an apartment that they need to rent here for eight months."

Then, she added, you have to consider all the living and travel expenses the players must dish out. "When Uncle Sam takes half," she continued, "it can go pretty quick in a lifestyle like this. So it still can be a struggle in the majors."

Mike Hargrove would readily agree. He said he and his wife had to stretch a small salary, renting "this attic from a lady for $15 a week. That is how my pro career began."

[*Baseball Digest*, 5/81]

Do the Indians "haze" their rookies?

Sure, that's a tradition, a rich part of the game. In 1995, amidst the loose atmosphere that goes with a winning season, Herbert Perry made it to the majors. Shortly after the last game of his first road trip with Cleveland to Toronto, he prepared to dress for the bus ride to the airport. That's when it hit him. He recalled, "**All of my clothes were missing from my locker. I had to wear these hobo clothes all the way back through the airport**. I swear I thought there was no way they [American customs officials] were going to let me back into the country."

Any classic tales of tormenting rookies?

One of the best stories comes from way back in 1975, when pitcher Fritz Peterson kept things loose in the

Indians' spring training locker room. A teammate of his, Duane Kuiper, looked back on a favorite trick. "Cy Buynak [the clubhouse attendant] would leave the weekly bill for clubhouse dues, say for $30, on players' chairs," said Kuiper. "Fritz put a '1' in front of the '30' on the rookies' bills. They'd see it and almost die! They didn't know anything, and they'd believe everything."

Have there been changes in the way rookies get treated?

Chris Chambliss said the hazing is dying down a bit. He said, "I think the game's a little bit different now—the money that they make now is so different. So some of those traditions have started to fade away."

He added that another rookie ordeal used to be having to serve the veterans when a group of players went out to eat. Of course, even eating out with a bunch of players, he says, is dying out. Players aren't together as much as they used to be, so, as he put it, "Some of those pranks don't really exist anymore."

Chambliss also pointed out that in the old days, "The older guys got more swings [in the batting cage] than the rookies, but nowadays everybody gets the same amount of swings because batting practice is so structured."

Pat Corrales says rookies now aren't put in their place the way they were long ago. When Corrales broke in, there was no cockiness or levity on the part of rookies. He recalled, "You kinda had to keep your mouth shut and do what you were told."

David Bell, a member of the 1995 and 1998 Indians, has

baseball roots that go back to the 1950s. His grandfather,
Gus, was a major leaguer, as was his father, Buddy. That
makes the Bell family the second of just three three-gener-
ation baseball families. Bell theorized on why rookies were
treated a lot more roughly in the old days. "Maybe guys
stayed with a team longer, and they developed more of a
close-knit thing where you had to break into their circle."
Bell, who once wore a skirt—much to the delight of
Cardinals veterans—concurs, "Guys *are* easier on rookies
now."

Rookie players get teased. How about rookie announcers?

Yes, according to Matt Underwood, but it's always "good
natured." The hazing, he says, "is earning your stripes, you
have to put your time in to get respect. Even a phenom is
still a rookie, Joe Charboneau proved that. You don't just
show up and have people fawn all over you. **You have
to prove you'll work hard, be diligent.
You have to earn the respect of players,
managers, and coaches**." Until then—and it can
take about a year—they will greet newcomers with a grin
and a "Hey, rookie."

Then do all rookies get teased—even, say, a batboy?

Yep, even a rookie batboy can't escape tricks. Indians
manager Mike Hargrove told the story of how Sutcliffe
would send a batboy looking for the key to the batter's box.
Everybody was in on the joke, and they'd send the kid on a
sort of wild scavenger hunt from clubhouse to clubhouse.
"Sometimes," said Hargrove, "we'd send a guy for a bag of

knuckleballs or curveballs." Did they truly fall for such stunts? "Sometimes," responded Hargrove with a smile. "It never hurt to try."

Do young players try to save some of their meal money?

Bill Selby said, "Yeah. Heck, I got a family and a house note [to pay on]. What I do a lot of times, since you spend a lot of money in clubhouse dues, I go over to the clubhouse and eat as much as I can over there. I go over there for lunch, get some early work done, eat dinner over there. Usually the only meal I buy is breakfast. That's what a clubhouse offers you in the big leagues—you have the option to do that, so why not take advantage of it? It's a chance to be smart with money, you don't have to go out and blow it."

MISCELLANEOUS

Does education give a ballplayer any advantage?

"I ain't afraid to tell the world that it don't take school stuff to help a fella play ball," said "Shoeless" Joe Jackson. [*Baseball's Greatest Quotations*]

Do some players shun the role of being a team leader?

Yes, said Ellis Burks. "There are certain issues that may be brought up that I'll have something to say about, but I don't consider myself a leader. I'm just part of the team. **If someone wants to talk to me about something, I'll talk to them, but I don't want to be a leader**." [*Elyria Chronicle Telegram*, 5/25/01]

What other aspects of the game do players take pride in?

Dennis Cook said that aside from making it to the majors, his most memorable moment was "My home run versus Fernando Valenzuela, a three-run shot. I got around the bases real quick, I was pretty excited. I was *so* excited, I went out the next inning and got shelled. **I went out thinking about the home run and not enough about pitching.**"

A former outfielder, he was proud of his hitting prowess. He had a couple of hits off Mike Scott when he was in his prime. "I hit his split-finger. I guarantee those guys pitched me like [they would] a hitter. I saw curves, changes, splits, fastballs—everything they threw."

Dave Otto's proudest moment was easy to remember. "My first big league win—seeing Steve Olin get the last three outs and me getting the win."

Other thoughts on pride?

Dennis Cook said, "I'm proudest of myself for just enduring. I've been down some rough roads and made it. Who would've thought a guy from a small town in Texas would even make it to the majors?" Especially since he was an 18th-round draft pick in 1985. More amazingly, as of the 2001 season, Cook was still producing as a 38-year-old big leaguer.

Can statistics be misleading?

They are often misleading. Two great quotes concerning stats came from former Indians. First from Bobby Bragen,

Cleveland's skipper in 1958 for 67 games. He once said, "Say you were standing with one foot in the oven and one foot in an ice bucket. According to the percentage people [statisticians], you should be [just] about perfectly comfortable." [*Baseball Quotations*]

Then there was the classic Toby Harrah comment: **"Statistics are a lot like a girl in a bikini. They reveal a lot, but not *everything*."**

Do young players worry about statistics more than experienced players?

As a rule, yes. Jack Armstrong put it this way, **"When you're younger, everything is predicated on stats. As you get older and more successful, you realize it's a team effort.** Then you are able to concentrate on each pitch rather than sweat each pitch."

Are the newer ballparks better than the old ones?

Paul Shuey said he is far from being a purist. "After you've been in Safeco, Jacobs, some of these new parks, you don't like the old parks—you don't like going to Fenway. **The tradition is there, but it's like you want to visit it, you don't want to pitch in it.**"

He finds that many of the older, smaller parks such as Fenway are even harder to pitch in now because the game is so oriented to offense these days. "If the game was the way it was back then [20 or more years ago], where pitchers were given a little more leeway here and there—the mounds were taller, balls were used more often so they were a little softer—shoot, you might like those parks a little better. But right now, you want them as big as you can find them, and you want as much room as possible." So, while he can't relate to a Fenway-like facility, he finds Detroit's Comerica to be fine.

Is there an aspect of the game that conservative veterans strongly dislike?

Travis Fryman replied, "I don't care for the flamboyance in all of professional sports today . . . It certainly doesn't elevate the individual, it only demeans them. . . It's perfectly all right to express your emotions, but not to the point where you disrespect others."

Meanwhile, Omar Vizquel thinks games last way too long. He said, **"If I had the power, I'd probably shorten the game to seven innings instead of nine."**

When a rookie has a great first season, does that make it tougher the second year?

Kenny Lofton refused to "buy that stuff about the sophomore jinx. **As a rookie, you don't know what's going on half the time. When you're in your second year, you should get even better because you know what to expect.** You know the pitchers and you know the league."

What don't most fans seem to realize about big league players?

"What people don't understand is we're just like them—we have a skill, that's our job, we're paid to be entertainers, but **we're everyday people just like anybody else except we get to play a game for a living**," said Bill Selby.

"A lot of people put baseball players on a pedestal, professional athletes in general, because they're on TV and you see them, but in all actuality they're no different from anybody else, they're just a gifted athlete," he said.

ACKNOWLEDGMENTS

A special thanks to all the good people associated with the Cleveland Indians who helped make my job easier, especially the fine folks in the media department: Susie Giuliano, Bart Swain, and Bob DiBiasio, Vice President of Public Relations. In addition, Mrs. Andrea Pacione-Thome gave up her a great deal of time to provide insight concerning the wives and the female side of the game. Of course, without the players, this project would have been doomed from the outset. So, an enormous thank-you is in order for the many Cleveland Indians who took the time to respond patiently to my questions. The 2000 edition of the Indians was a fine group to work with, a class organization from top to bottom. Players were so cooperative that writing this book was a joy.

Likewise, a large thanks goes out to the staff of Gray and Company, Publishers. Their help, ideas, and insights were so valuable.

BIBLIOGRAPHY

Allen, Lee. *The American League Story*. New York: Hill, 1962.

Boudreau, Lou, with Russell Schneider. *Covering All the Bases*. Champaign: Sagamore Publishing, 1993.

Cleveland Indians Media Guide. Cleveland: Cleveland Indians, 2000.

Connor, Anthony J. *Baseball For the Love Of It*: Collier Books, 1984.

Davis, Hank. *Small Town Heroes: Images of Minor League Baseball*. Iowa City: University of Iowa Press, 1997.

Dickson, Paul. *Baseball's Greatest Quotations*. NY: Harper Collins, 1991.

Feller, Bob with Burton Rocks. *Bob Feller's Little Black Book of Baseball Wisdom*. Chicago: Contemporary Books, 2001.

Feller, Bob, with Bill Gilbert. *Now Pitching: A Baseball Memoir*. New York: Carol Publishing Group, 1990.

Franklin, Pete with Terry Pluto. *You Could Argue But You'd Be Wrong*. Chicago: Contemporary Books, 1988.

Hargrove, Sharon. *Safe at Home: A Baseball Wife's Story*. Costa College Station: Texas A&M University Press, 1989.

Jedick, Peter. *League Park*. Cleveland: P. Jedick, 1978.

Long, Tim. *Indians Memories*. Cleveland: Gray & Company, 1997.

Lowry, Philip J. *Green Cathedrals*. Reading: Addison-Wesley Pub. Co., 1992.

Moffi, Larry. *This Side of Cooperstown*. Iowa City: University of Iowa, 1996.

Nathan, David. *Baseball Quotations*. Jefferson, NC: McFarland, 1991.

Paige, Satchel with Hal Lebovitz. *Pitchin' Man*. Cleveland: Hal Lebovitz, 1948.

Pluto, Terry. *The Curse of Rocky Colavito: A Loving Look at a Thirty-Year Slump*. New York: Simon & Schuster, 1994.

———. *Our Tribe: A Baseball Memoir*. New York: Simon & Schuster, 1999.

Schneider, Russell. *The Boys of the Summer of '48*. Champaign: Sports Pub., 1998.

———. *The Cleveland Indians Encyclopedia*. Philadelphia: Temple University Press, 1996.

———. *Tribe Memories: The First Century*. Hinckley: Moonlight Publishing, 2000

Stewart, Wayne. *Baseball Bafflers*. New York: Sterling Pub. Co., 1999.

———. *Baseball Oddities*. New York: Sterling Pub. Co., 1998.

———. *Baseball Puzzlers: You Make the Call*. New York: Sterling Pub., 2000.

Torry, Jack. *Endless Summers: The Fall and Rise of the Cleveland Indians*. South Bend: Diamond Communications, Inc. 1995

Vecsey, George. *Joy in Mudville*. New York: McCall Pub. Co., 1970.

Veeck, Bill with Ed Linn. *Veeck as in Wreck*. NY: Putnam, 1962.

INDEX

Cleveland Guides & Gifts

More good books from Gray & Company ...

If you enjoyed this book, try one of these other great books about Cleveland ...

Indians Memories / A nostalgic roller coaster ride including laughably bad seasons and two exciting eras of championship baseball. *Tim Long* / $5.95 softcover

On Being Brown / Thoughtful essays and interviews exploring what it means to be a true fan of the Cleveland Browns. *Scott Huler* / $18.95 hardcover, $10.95 softcover

Cleveland Sports Trivia Quiz / Test your knowledge with these 500 brain-teasing questions and answers on all kinds of Cleveland sports. *Tim Long* / $6.95 softcover

Cleveland Golfer's Bible / All of Greater Cleveland's golf courses and driving ranges are described in this essential guide for any golfer. *John Tidyman* / $13.95 softcover

Cleveland Fishing Guide / Best public fishing spots in Northeast Ohio, what kind of fish you'll find, and how to catch them. Directory of fishing resources. *John Barbo* / $13.95 softcover

Cleveland On Foot
Beyond Cleveland On Foot / Two books of self-guided walking tours: first, through Greater Cleveland's neighborhoods, suburbs, and metroparks; then, through parks and small towns of 7 neighboring counties. *Patience Cameron Hoskins* / $14.95 softcover

Neil Zurcher's Favorite One Tank Trips (Book 1)
More of Neil Zurcher's One Tank Trips (Book 2)
One Tank Trips Road Food (Book 3)
If you enjoyed Neil's first book of One Tank Trips, you'll love discovering hundreds more unusual nearby getaway ideas in his next two books. / $13.95 softcover (each)

Dick Goddard's Weather Guide for Northeast Ohio / Seasonal facts, folklore, storm tips, and weather wit from Cleveland's top meteorologist. / $13.95 softcover

Cleveland Family Fun / 441 great ideas for places to go and things to do with kids of all ages. Written by parents, for parents. *Jennifer Stoffel* / $13.95 softcover

365 Ways to Meet People in Cleveland / Friendship, romance, and networking ideas for singles, couples, and families. *Miriam Carey* / $8.95 softcover

52 Romantic Outings in Greater Cleveland / Easy-to-follow "recipes" for romance, for a lunch hour, an evening, or a full day together. *Miriam Carey* / $13.95 softcover

Cleveland Ethnic Eats / Discover Cleveland's authentic ethnic restaurants and markets and taste the exotic flavors of the world without leaving town! *Laura Taxel* / $13.95 softcover

Cleveland Cemeteries / Meet Cleveland's most interesting "permanent" residents in these 61 outdoor history parks. *Vicki Blum Vigil* / $13.95 softcover

Photo from *Cleveland: A Portrait of the City*, by Jonathan Wayne   **Continued ...**

They Died Crawling and Other Tales
The Maniac in the Bushes
The Corpse in the Cellar / Three collections of gripping true tales about Cleveland crimes and disasters. Include spine-chilling photos. *John Stark Bellamy* / $13.95 softcover (each)

Cleveland: A Portrait / 105 color photographs capture Greater Cleveland's landmarks and hidden details in all seasons. *Jonathan Wayne* / $35.00 hardcover *(photo above is from this book.)*

What's So Big About Cleveland, Ohio? / What does a well-traveled 10-year-old think about her first visit to Cleveland? "B-o-o-o-ring". Until, that is, she discovers a very special little secret … *Sara Holbrook & Ennis McNulty* / $17.95 hardcover

Ghoulardi / The behind-the-scenes story of Cleveland's wildest TV legend. Rare photos, interviews, show transcripts, and Ghoulardi trivia. *Tom Feran & R. D. Heldenfels* / $17.95 softcover

The Ghoul Scrapbook / Rare photos, show transcripts, and video captures from "The Main Maniac" of Cleveland late-night TV. *Ron Sweed & Mike Olszewski* / $17.95 softcover

Feagler's Cleveland / The best from three decades of commentary by Cleveland's top columnist, Dick Feagler. Witty, insightful, opinionated, thoughtful. / $13.95 softcover

"Did You Read Feagler Today?" / The most talked about recent columns by Cleveland's most outspoken columnist. / $13.95 softcover

Barnaby and Me / Linn Sheldon, a Cleveland TV legend as "Barnaby", tells the fascinating story of his own extraordinary life. / $20.00 hardcover

The Great Indoors / The first decade of Eric Broder's hilarious weekly "Great Indoors" column. Reread favorites, or get caught up with the ongoing saga. / $13.95 softcover

Cleveland TV Memories / Remember when TV was local? A nostalgic collection of 365 favorite local shows, hosts, jingles, bloopers, stunts, and more. *Feran & Heldenfels* / $6.95 softcover

Bed & Breakfast Getaways from Cleveland / 80 charming small inns perfect for an easy weekend or evening away from home. *Doris Larson* / $13.95 softcover

The Cleveland Orchestra Story / How a midwestern orchestra became a titan in the world of classical music. With 102 rare photographs. *Donald Rosenberg* / $40.00 hardcover

Cleveland Garden Handbook / Local experts tell how to grow a beautiful garden in Northeast Ohio. Filled with practical tips. *Susan McClure* / $12.95

Available at your local bookstore.

These books are stocked at Northeast Ohio bookstores, are available from most online book retailers, and can be ordered at any bookstore in the U.S.

Need help finding a retailer near you? Call us toll-free: **1-800-915-3609**.

Gray & Company, Publishers
1588 E. 40th St., Cleveland, OH 44103 / 216-431-2665

for more information, visit: **www.grayco.com**